How to Set Up and Run
a Payroll System

How to Set Up and Run a
PAYROLL SYSTEM

Carol Anderson

KOGAN
PAGE

First published in Great Britain in 1990 by
Kogan Page Limited, 120 Pentonville Road,
London N1 9JN.

Editorial packaging by Redfern Publishing Services,
Kenilworth, Warwickshire

While every care has been taken to ensure the accuracy
of the contents of this work, no responsibility for loss
occasioned to any person acting or refraining from
action as a result of any statement in it can be
accepted by the author, packager or publisher.

British Library Cataloguing in Publication Data
Anderson, Carol
  How to set up and run a payroll system.
  1. Great Britain. Personnel. Remuneration. Management
  aspects
  I. Title
  658.3'2'0941

  ISBN 1-85091-954-2
  ISBN 1-85091-955-0 pbk

Typeset by DP Photosetting, Aylesbury, Bucks
Printed and bound in Great Britain by
Biddles Ltd, Guildford

Contents

90; Periods of Incapacity for Work (PIW) 91; Employees for whom no SSP can be paid 92; Waiting days 94; Payment of SSP 96; Deductions from SSP 98; Mistakes in SSP calculations or payments and how to reclaim SSP and NIC 98; What to do when SSP stops 99; Record-keeping 100; Control of absences due to sickness 101; Offences and penalties 101

Acknowledgements

I would like to thank Jim Yuill for guidance on National Insurance, Statutory Sick Pay and Statutory Maternity Pay, and Teresa and Jenny for typing the manuscript.

I would also like to thank the Controller of Her Majesty's Stationery Office for giving permission to reproduce the Inland Revenue and Department of Social Security forms, tables and flow charts.

Preface

The operation of Pay As You Earn (PAYE) is the same whether an organisation employs one or one thousand employees. The basic rules apply whether the business is run by a sole trader, such as a shop or service provider, by a partnership such as a firm of solicitors, accountants or dentists, or a limited company, ranging from small family firms to large public limited companies. This book can therefore be used as a basic, practical guide by any business which employs people.

Most of the guidance produced for employers is issued in booklet form by two government departments, The Inland Revenue and Department of Social Security. Although these booklets are now marginally easier to understand, they contain no practical advice for employers on the methods that can be used to process payroll, or what the most common problems are and how to avoid them. Indeed, the employer not only has to understand officialdom's regulations but also know how to communicate with the authorities, investigate the procedures necessary in following out the two departments' rules, and know what actions to take in order to reclaim overpayment.

This book sets out in simple language the basic rules for PAYE – what to do and when to do it. It contains practical tips and information to aid the employer or his payroll office and so facilitate the smooth running of the payroll system.

Throughout the book the masculine gender 'he' has been used, except in instances where it clearly requires the use of 'she'.

Introduction

As soon as a businessman can no longer carry out by himself all the work he acquires, he needs a payroll system to pay the wages of his first employee. It is a fact of life that there is no simple way of operating Pay As You Earn (PAYE): if you have to set up a payroll system the rules are exactly the same regardless of the number of employees. The only thing that changes is how many times the calculations need to be repeated.

The operation of PAYE was introduced during the Second World War. Until then employers had been operating a simplified National Insurance system for employees, but wage-earners paid their own income tax in two half-yearly instalments, based on an assessment issued by their local tax office. The introduction of PAYE meant that all employers had to calculate and deduct income tax from wages, pay the net wage to the employee and account for the tax deducted to the Inland Revenue each month, and then balance the books at the end of each tax year. Employers had become unpaid tax collectors.

The system by which employers deduct income tax has changed little since its inception. An employee makes a claim for tax-free allowances, for example the married man's allowance, and the total of the allowances is converted to a code by the tax office and issued to the employer. The employer uses the codes sent to him to determine the weekly or monthly tax-free pay that can be deducted from the 'gross' amount to be paid, and then looks up in tables the amount of tax each employee should pay on 'taxable' earnings.

There have been many changes in the operation of the National Insurance system for employees: it is no longer necessary for employers to keep a card for each wage-earner and purchase National Insurance stamps of the right value each week, attach them to the cards and send them to the Department of Social Security (DSS) (previously the DHSS) when full. The correct amount of National Insurance (NI) is found by looking up an employee's earnings which are subject to NI in one of a set of tables issued by the DSS. There are far more statistics to be kept than in the past and the matter is complicated further by changes in the nature of earnings that the DSS consider to attract NI.

Both government departments, the DSS and the Inland Revenue, involved in PAYE (a term that includes income tax and NI) have become more assertive in their roles as revenue gatherers, and recent years have seen more investigations undertaken to ensure that employers not only operate PAYE, but do it correctly, so that no income is lost to the Exchequer. This means that as the system becomes more complicated, and operators of that system more likely to make mistakes, both the Inland Revenue and the DSS are using their resources to find errors, collect underpaid tax and NI, and penalise employers for making the errors. The tax and NI income to the Exchequer is so enormous that it is a very profitable exercise for underpaid duties to be found and collected.

However, the government departments will not seek further tax from employers without first establishing whether an underpayment has occurred; of course, once established, there are few acceptable reasons why the full amounts should not have been paid. If members of the general public, ie employers, are to act as unpaid tax collectors, then what they do must be clearly laid down in law for everybody's protection, and the law in relation to PAYE firmly puts the onus on employers, not only to operate the system, but also to take reasonable care in operating it. Put simply, this means that employers, when they deduct tax and NI etc, have a duty to get it right. There are few problems with clearly identified amounts of wages or salary paid to obvious employees, but there are many problems with 'payments-in-kind' instead of in cash, and also where there may be some difference of opinion regarding the status of the employee, for example a casual or self-employed worker.

Since the introduction of PAYE, some employers have tried to avoid their responsibilities. There have been many reasons for this, most of them related to the employer's or the employee's money. In many cases, however, it is due to the fact that a payroll officer or department is an expense which earns nothing for the business, and therefore no employer will feel inclined to spend hard-earned money on equipping for payroll, or on recruiting and training expensive staff. The end-of-the-month sales figures are vital to a sales-orientated company, but as long as the pay has gone in the bank, nobody is very interested in how it got there.

Over the last few years the DSS have considered the most cost-effective ways of paying state benefits to individuals. It seemed reasonable to assume that as employers already had the machinery to pay wages and make complicated deductions of tax and NI, they could also take on the administration of state benefit payments. Since April 1983 employers have been responsible for calculating and paying Statutory Sick Pay (SSP) to their employees, and as the operation of this new system was satisfactory, from April 1978 employers were also required to make payments of Statutory Maternity Pay (SMP).

Thus the wages clerk who 40 years ago learnt the complexities of PAYE is clearly far removed from the technician of today who needs to know and understand a whole range of legislation and procedures, and who is probably able to use a computer to assist in the task.

The computer is now firmly established in payroll. Because of the necessary complex calculations, using tables, percentages and identifiable categories of payments or people, it is clearly an area where a computer is valuable. Indeed, before computers were a standard item in most businesses it was usual to see a range of adding machines, comptometers and calculating machines, in payroll offices. It must not be forgotten that a computer calculates on the data that is put into it, and the modern phrase GIGO (garbage in, garbage out) applies to payroll as to other areas of business. The computer cannot operate PAYE correctly unless all payments and people who should be in the system are entered in it. Thus, even the best computer system is no guarantee of accurate PAYE operation. The data processed may be accurate, but the data omitted may well give rise to underpayments of revenue which could be found by the DSS or Inland Revenue audit teams.

If decisions have to be made about what and who are subject to PAYE, then it is necessary to ensure that the staff making those decisions are well versed in the NI and Inland Revenue rules and are prepared to keep records up to date. If in any doubt, the safest decision is to subject that particular person or payment to PAYE. In the event of there being an overpayment, a refund is always possible; if, however, there is an underpayment, the employer will usually be asked to settle both his and the employee's liability, together with a penalty and, under the latest legislation, interest as well.

This book is intended to be easily understood, even by someone new to payroll. It is hoped that it will be as quick and easy for an employer or payroll officer to refer to it for exact information as required, as it would be to 'ask Flossie' who has 30 years' experience. 'Flossies' are wonderful founts of knowledge, but many are, in practice, still reciting rules of yesteryear, and are sadly not up to date with current thinking. The rules for all government deductions and payments are explained as simply as possible and information is given in the form of positive instructions without leaving you in any doubt as to the correct course of action to take.

In addition to statutory obligations, the book covers areas where employers have a choice of action. It gives guidance, for instance, on the simplest way of making expense payments. It also covers the question of computerisation of payroll, giving the areas to analyse which will help in making a well-reasoned decision of whether or not to computerise your payroll system.

All areas of payroll are covered, and payroll management is also looked at. This comprehensive guide can be used for all types of business.

Part One:
Income Tax

1

Becoming an Employer for the First Time

Before you inform the statutory authorities of your intention to become an employer you should make sure that your letter box is large enough to take the torrent of literature that will be sent to you. A letter to *The Times* in July 1988 recorded that a new employer had been sent some 30 different documents, totalling 503 pages, and all for one employee!

Your first action must be to inform your local tax office that you intend to take on an employee. In response, they will send you a 'starter pack' which *should* contain all the information you need in order to operate PAYE. It should include tax tables, information leaflets on both income tax and National Insurance contributions (NIC), deduction working sheets and other forms, reference numbers of which will be noted throughout this book. The implied reservation is deliberate as it depends on what forms, leaflets and so on that particular tax office has available at that time.

If the sight of all the books and leaflets is too daunting and you feel that you really cannot run your business and be a tax collector at the same time, then you may be best advised to ask your accountant to do all the work for you.

The second piece of advice (apart from not to have any employees) is to find time to deal with payroll. The Pay As You Earn (PAYE) system is very complex when seen as a whole, but is much more reasonable when sections are looked at individually. If you need to pay people on a Friday, do not leave the calculations until after lunch on that day. The sight of a posse of hopeful employees in happy anticipation of large pay packets for the weekend does not allow for the quiet concentration which is needed in order to finish the job.

The tax office will inform the Collector of Taxes of your new status and will send your new employer's reference number to you. This should be used each time you pay money in, together with a book of payslips to be used monthly when making your payments to the Collector.

The DSS will not normally issue you with NI tables when you start to employ people, but should these not be included in the starter pack from your local tax office, you can obtain copies from your DSS office. The money you collect as National Insurance (NI) contributions is sent to the Collector along with income tax deductions, so you do not have a Department of Social Security (DSS) employer's number that is different from your Collector of Taxes' number.

Your wages records form part of your normal business records, so your accountant will need to look at them at the end of your accounting year. The records you need to keep are dealt with more fully in Part Four. Like any other record of transactions, it will be easier for you or your payroll staff or accountant to follow what has happened if the records are neat, tidy and up to date. This will save time in finding errors when auditing takes place, and time, of course, is money – your money.

Setting up the system

You will need to make several decisions before your first pay date, such as frequency of payment and method of paying people. Your employees may wish to have some say in the matter, but if you have already decided on a system to suit your business, then most employees will probably agree to it.

It is more and more common each year for employees to be paid by cheque or bank transfer. Since the abolition of the Truck Acts in 1986, payment in cash can no longer be insisted upon by new employees, so do not offer it. The transport of cash is a dangerous and expensive operation so it is advisable to avoid it if you can. Larger employers have the option to pay automatically by BACS (Bankers' Automated Clearing System) and this system is discussed in Part Five.

The operation of PAYE is a time-consuming task, and the calculations are very similar whether you pay people weekly or monthly. If at all possible, new employees should be paid at monthly intervals so that these calculations have to be performed only 12 times a year, instead of the 52 calculations needed for weekly paid people.

Employees paid weekly or in cash will usually seek an incentive payment from their employer when a change to monthly payments or bank transfers is sought. You will avoid this expense, and the negotiations that go with it, if you set the rules you want from the start. It sometimes happens that if trade unions become involved in the negotiations, the members may accept terms which allow a concession, such as monthly payments being paid on the twenty-fifth day of each month instead of on the last day.

You may have less choice, depending on the category of work done, on hourly rates, piece work, etc, but as these add more complications to the system they should be avoided in order to operate an easier payroll system. If you need to pay complicated rates, then it is worth paying a standard rate on the first pay-day, and include overtime, or whatever, in the next month's pay packet, when there has been time to check and process the data. In this way employees will receive full pay for each pay period except the first, and will receive an extra payment of the final amounts of overtime, etc, after they leave. If employees are reluctant to accept payment in arrears, it is usually acceptable to pay an advance of salary with the first payment that will roughly equal the extra payment due the next pay-day. The advance can then be adjusted either each pay-day or when an employee leaves.

2
The Tax Year

The Pay As You Earn (PAYE) year, for various reasons, starts on 6 April and ends on the following 5 April. The tax year 1991/92 starts on 6 April 1991 and ends on 5 April 1992. At the end of each tax year summaries are made of all payments and deductions, and end-of-year returns are submitted to the Inland Revenue for tax, National Insurance (NI), Statutory Sick Pay (SSP), and Statutory Maternity Pay (SMP) (see Part Four).

Monthly-paid employees have 12 pay-days in a tax year, normally 30 April to 31 March inclusive, or whatever day of the month you choose to pay on. Weekly-paid employees normally have 52 pay days; their first pay-day falls in the week beginning 6 April, and their last pay-day in the tax year in the week ending on 5 April. It is the actual date of payment that determines which tax period is to be used to calculate income tax.

The standard year has 365 days, and a leap year 366 days, so sometimes with weekly-paid people you will have used all the 52 weeks available and still have another pay-day on 4/5 April. These dates must still be included in the tax year ending on 5 April, so there is a special system to deal with these payments which is described in Part Four. You will, of course, avoid this complication if all employees are paid monthly.

The tax week or month to be used for a particular pay-day can be found by looking at the calendar in the first few pages of the *Employer's Guide to PAYE* (booklet P7) or in the tax-free pay tables at the head of each page.

Tax codes

Each individual resident in the UK is entitled to income tax allowances, based on his personal circumstances. These are usually allocated for employees by the tax office which deals with you as an employer. The amount of personal allowance given is the amount of the earnings the individual can earn in that particular year before income tax is calculated.

22

The allowances are therefore the tax-free pay of the employee. In order to operate PAYE at intervals throughout the year, a proportion of the allowances due is given by an amount of tax-free pay each week or month. The tax office converts allowances into a code for each individual and notifies the employer of that code which must be used until a new one is issued.

Most codes are operated cumulatively, so that the free pay at month 1 will equal one-twelfth of the allowances due for the year, for month 2, two-twelfths, and so on; therefore by month 12, an employee will have received free pay equal to the full amount of the allowances due for the year. If free pay is cumulative, then so too must the pay be against which this is set. Totals are made each pay-day of gross pay to date, so that total free pay to date can be deducted from it to give total taxable pay to date.

There will be times when it would not be correct to use the normal cumulative basis, and in these cases a 'week 1' or 'month 1' basis is used. This simply means that tax is worked out each week as if it were week 1 of the tax year, and no cumulative totals are used. The tax office will tell you if they wish you to use this non-cumulative system, or sometimes you will need to make this decision for new employees (see Chapter 5).

Emergency code

There are occasions, for instance, when the tax office have not issued you with a code for an employee, and therefore you will need to use a temporary code called an emergency code. This code can be used, for example, for new employees. It gives a single person's tax allowance on a 'Week 1' basis. The rules for codes to be given to new employees are described in Chapter 5.

Tax tables

Each pay-day, the employer will have computed the gross pay due to an employee, and will need to find out how much of that pay is 'tax-free', how much is 'taxable pay', and what amount of tax should be deducted. This is done by using free-pay and taxable-pay tables which will have been issued with the employer's starter pack. The free-pay tables give the amount of tax-free pay for each pay period throughout the year and by using the employee's code his free-pay can be ascertained. Should you have a new employee, previously unemployed for some time, then the benefit of the free-pay unused for those unemployed weeks or months will normally be taken into account when the cumulative system is used.

Once the free pay for the pay period has been determined (by deducting this figure from gross pay), the taxable pay figure is obtained. The amount of taxable pay is found in the taxable pay tables and this will show the tax due. Fuller instructions are given in Part Four.

The tax tables are designed to deal with all rates of income tax, and also changes in rates made in the Chancellor's Budget. If rates of tax change in the Budget, then new tables are issued to employers automatically with instructions on how and when to use them. It is common for income tax allowances also to be increased in the Budget, and details of these increases will be issued to employers on Form P7X, together with guidance notes.

3
Who is an Employee?

The Pay As You Earn (PAYE) system includes all employees and office-holders, which means that directors of limited companies are employees of their own companies. It can be difficult on occasions to decide whether someone is an employee of yours or working on their own account. The difference – and a very important one at that – is whether there is a 'Contract of Service', as in the case of an employee, or a 'Contract for Services' as between a business and a self-employed person.

The PAYE system imposes a statutory duty on employers to operate PAYE for their employees, and there are often differences of opinion about the status of certain 'employees'. This can mean that an employer will decide that a particular person is self-employed, make no PAYE deductions, and some months or years later the Inland Revenue could decide, on the facts available to them, that the person was an employee and ask the employer to pay to them all the under-deducted sums. Because it is the duty of the employer to make deductions when necessary, if he fails in that duty, the Revenue would not seek to recover the sums due from the employee but from the employer. It can therefore be very expensive for employers to make wrong decisions in this matter.

There are several factors to be taken into account when deciding the status of an employee, and these include such matters as:

- On whose premises is the work done, and with whose equipment?
- Under whose day-to-day control does the person work?
- Is holiday and sick pay paid, and is the person in the company pension scheme?
- Is the person incurring any financial risk, or exercising their own managerial skills and judgement?

It is not enough for an employer and an employee simply to decide that for convenience sake the employee will be classed as self-employed when the facts suggest otherwise. You are advised in cases of doubt to ask your local tax office for guidance, or at least to obtain from the self-employed person confirmation from his tax office of his self-employed status.

Your tax office will let you have leaflet IR56 which sets out many of the pointers to consider, and you could give this to the employee who considers himself to be self-employed and await his comments. In the meantime, of course, you should continue to deduct PAYE.

When you have accepted the obligation to operate PAYE, you will need to know whether any special treatment applies in some cases. If you are in any doubt about what to do in the case of a new employee you should refer to Chapter 5 which details the steps to be taken.

Students

Not all students qualify for special tax treatment under PAYE, so you need to consider factors other than simply that the person is at college. Students are taxable personnel, but because they tend to earn their money during the holiday periods, they can, in effect, have all their tax-free allowances for the year bunched together for, say, the summer vacation. If a student's tax-free allowances were £2500 for the year, then he could earn the whole of that amount in 10 weeks at £250 per week. You need not deduct tax from the pay of a student working for you provided the following conditions are satisfied:

1. The student must work for you in the holidays only. If work is done at any other time, the student will not qualify for this special treatment.
2. You must give the student Form P38(S) which must be completed, signed and returned to you. The student confirms that his income for the tax year will not exceed the figure on the form.
3. The student must be attending a UK university, college or polytechnic, and not be on a course abroad and home for the holidays.

You should also note the following points. If the Easter holiday covers the end of the tax year (5/6 April), then you will need to ask the student to sign a new Form P38(S) for the new tax year. Students not on courses in the UK will be taxed in the normal way unless, very rarely, they bring a different Form P38(S) already stamped by BUNAC or CFS/AOSC which are North American or Canadian student organisations. There is no special treatment for students for National Insurance (NI) purposes; you follow the normal rules as set out in Chapter 7.

Pensioners

Pensioners' income is taxable, and although they often object strongly, the UK income tax system includes them. When a past Chancellor of the Exchequer was questioned on this point, he simply stated that income tax was a tax on income, and pensioners had income whether from pensions or any other source. (When asked about this point during lectures, I have a simple answer: to decide whether a person is taxable ask one question – is he breathing? – if he is, he is liable for income tax. The general rule to remember is that all individuals in the UK are taxable entities, and they only escape tax where particular rules or concessions apply, for example where income does not exceed the personal allowance given by the authority.)

If you employ a pensioner, you must treat him in exactly the same way as other employees for PAYE. Whatever special rules there may be in relation to levels of income and payment of the Statutory Retirement Pension (SRP), these do not affect the taxation of income.

If an employee retires from your company, you may pay him a pension in respect of his years of service with you. If you are paying this pension, then you need to carry on the operation of PAYE on that pension. The first thing to do is to send Form P160 to your tax office, and then start making tax deductions from the pension using the pensioner's current code, but changing it from a cumulative basis to a week 1 or month 1 basis. More usually these days, pensions are paid by pension fund trustees, and if this is the case, you will need to issue Form P45 when the pensioner leaves your employment. Write the word 'pensioner' at the top of part 1 of the form before sending it to the tax office.

You could, of course, continue to employ the retired person even though he may be receiving a pension from you. In this case you need not issue Form P45, but let your tax office know what is happening by letter. More usually, the existing contract of employment will have been terminated at retirement, and it may be clearer to everyone concerned if the Form P45 was issued and on it noted 're-engaged pensioner'. If you were to re-engage that person as a self-employed consultant, the guidance at the start of this chapter on the rules of self-employment should be carefully considered.

Employees working abroad

Just because an employee works abroad it does not necessarily mean that he is exempt from UK tax. If an employee leaves his job with you to work abroad, then you treat this as an employee leaving in the normal way.

If one of your employees is going abroad to work for you, then you should in the first instance continue to make normal PAYE deductions. The employee should get in touch with the tax office (where he sends his returns) if the period abroad is likely to exceed one year, as there may be a special concession for the earnings while abroad, and for other income in the UK also if the period abroad exceeds a complete tax year. This concession depends on complicated tax rules, and as the benefit of the special treatment is exemption from tax for earnings while abroad, it is very worthwhile making sure the rules in relation to visits home are complied with. A total of days spent abroad, together with days in the UK, needs to be kept from the start of the period abroad, and visits to the UK must be timed so that they do not break these rules. It is often worth obtaining professional advice, as large sums of money can be at stake in these circumstances.

A foreign Revenue authority may contact you in connection with your employees abroad, and ask you to make foreign tax deductions for them. If this happens you should explain that you are still responsible for PAYE deductions in this country, and ask why they consider foreign tax is payable. You may then forward their reply to your tax office and ask for instructions.

Employees in offshore areas

The normal PAYE system applies for most employees working offshore, for example in the North Sea oil and gas fields. However, there are exceptions, for example special rules apply for divers. You should therefore ask your tax office for advice detailing the particular circumstances in *each* case. If employees move around while offshore, you should notify the tax office of these changes in area.

Employees from abroad

When an employee comes to the UK to work for you, you will normally need to deduct tax, treating the employee as a new starter. Individuals will sometimes suggest to employers that as they will only be in the UK for a short time before moving on, no deductions will need to be made! You will, of course, discount this suggestion, knowing by now that it is your duty to operate PAYE against all employees' wages. If any exemptions are due, the tax office will let you know *after* the employee has made contact with the Inland Revenue.

You may still be liable for PAYE even in the event of the employee being employed by a foreign company while working for you. Such liability occurs if you provide the general control and management of that employee, or if you operate the UK branch or office of that overseas company. You should find out the earnings being paid by the foreign company and ask them to deduct PAYE from those earnings. You may then recover these amounts from any charge made to you by the overseas company for the services provided. You may ask your tax office for a ruling if you consider any employee from abroad not to be working within your company's control and management.

Employees with more than one job

An employee applying for a job will not always admit that he already has one. Therefore, you should follow the procedure for new employees and operate PAYE as normal, as you cannot assume that the other employer will make deductions for both of you. If tax will be overpaid by the employee, the tax office can adjust matters if they are informed. There are many people with a number of jobs who avoid paying tax and NI and who come within the so-called 'Black Economy'. The Inland Revenue have special teams around the country whose job is to try to find these people, and to encourage employers to operate PAYE (the penalty for not correctly dealing with a new employee's PAYE has been increased from £50 to £300). Some employers have been avoiding the problem by grossing up payments to 'casual' employees, so that the net, after tax and NI deductions, is the agreed amount of pay for the job which, of course, is more expensive. The new penalty level is certain to be an encouragement to those employers to ensure all employees are dealt with correctly.

Part-time and casual workers

Nowadays there is little distinction between types of employee for PAYE purposes. The belief that deductions need not be made from some of your work-force because, for example, they are only casuals, will not be correct. These people are still considered to be your employees and the normal procedures should be followed when they first work for you. The penalties for not operating PAYE correctly for new employees is mentioned in the section above, and should be taken seriously.

You should always ask any employee for his copy of the Form P45 given by the last employer and, if this is provided, you follow the procedures in Chapter 5. If no Form P45 is handed in, a different set procedure is followed.

Guidance for employees who have no Form P45 is given in paragraph

D43 of the *Employer's Guide to PAYE* (booklet number P7). Table A is for employees who are going to work for you for more than one week; and Table B is for employees who are going to work for you for less than one week. You should follow the instructions on the flow charts, deducting tax and NI where appropriate. It is a popular misconception that all new employees have tax deductions worked out using the emergency code. This basis can be used where the employee can certify that he has just left school, or that this employment is his only or main job.

Some casual employees assume that PAYE deductions will not be made from their pay, and complain when you make them. The areas in which tax-free payments are likely to be made are steadily decreasing, as employers are either discovered by the Inland Revenue and asked to pay the tax, or businesses become more aware of their responsibilities and the penalties for ignoring them. If it is really necessary to pay people so that they avoid the correct deductions, then you can do this by grossing up the pay for the tax and NI due, making the correct deductions, and paying the 'net' to these employees. This keeps the employee and Inland Revenue happy, but, of course, increases your wage bill considerably.

Agency workers

It can be useful to most businesses to use the services of an agency to provide temporary staff, particularly when the requirement will be for a limited duration. If workers are supplied through a recognised UK agency, then that agency will be responsible for operating PAYE on the fees it pays to those staff. If your company is operating as an agency and supplying workers for other companies, then you will be responsible for the PAYE deductions, even though you may feel that the workers you supply are working for the fee-paying company and not for you.

If you pay any money to agency workers direct, whether for pay or expenses, then you should operate PAYE on those amounts. You should also operate PAYE where the worker asks you to pay someone other than the agency, or that agency is outside the UK. If you are in any doubt as to whether deductions should be withheld, then you should ask your tax office for advice.

Directors and certain employees

Until recently the above heading would have read 'Directors and higher-paid employees', but from 6 April 1989 it is accepted by the Inland Revenue that people earning at a rate of £8500 a year are not now 'higher-paid', and this category has now been renamed 'certain employees'.

The first point to remember is that company directors are employees and PAYE deductions should be made as normal. Directors in particular have had a long-standing belief that PAYE should not apply to them, but Inland Revenue compliance units have been spreading the word for some time now that it does. Directors have for many years been assessed for income tax on their income on the 'earnings basis'. They have argued that their directors' fees were not earned until voted to them in the accounts of the company, but this procedure often occurred many months after they had actually drawn the cash to live on. The compliance teams have tried to ensure that the companies in question complied with PAYE making deductions when amounts were paid or drawn from the company. In his Budget of March 1989, the Chancellor of the Exchequer made the correct basis of assessment for earnings the 'receipts basis'. This will give more strength to the compliance teams' tasks. You should, therefore, operate PAYE on directors' pay, whether salary, fees or bonus at the time that the director becomes entitled to the money which is withdrawn from the company, and even when money is drawn on account of fees, etc.

It is perhaps useful here to pay some attention to definitions. The term 'director' in *this* instance means a company director, a person who owns shares in the company, and not an ordinary employee whose title includes the executive term 'director', for example 'sales director'. There are many complicated issues concerning directors and a number of definitions of the word 'director', and professional advice is required to make sure that special provisions are complied with. For example, NI for company directors is very different from that for other employees (see Chapter 7 for further information).

The definition of a 'certain employee' is one whose total of earnings, expenses and benefits for a tax year is at an annual rate exceeding £8500. Special rules apply to company directors, whatever their rate of pay, and these certain employees, so it is important to identify them correctly. Where an employee's pay in that year is, for example, £8000 and he is in receipt of benefits and expenses totalling £600, then his annual rate of pay is in excess of £8500 and as such is within the special rules. The definition gives an annual rate of pay, which means that an employee who starts or leaves your employment during the year needs to be given special consideration. For example, an employee who leaves at the end of June (tax year commences 6 April) having earned £3000 will have actual pay below the £8500 limit, but an annualised salary of £12,000.

At the end of each year a return of pay, tax deductions and NI contributions have to be made, and for this special category of employees a further return has to be made on Form P11D. This is a return of all expenses payments and benefits for the year. The Inland Revenue give guidance in booklet 480 *Notes on Expenses Payments and Benefits for Directors and Certain Employees*. Many employers these days have reached the position where all their employees are within this special category and so this additional return has to be made for the whole workforce. Any employee not within this definition may still need a return of a limited range of expenses and benefits on Form P9D, see Chapter 15 for the items described on that form.

Expenses and benefits in kind

An employer is required to give details to the tax office on Form P11D of any amount of expenses payments for travelling and subsistence, etc, and benefits in kind, such as cars or private medical insurance, and virtually anything else of value which an employer gives to employees as part of their reward for work done.

Some years ago it was possible for employers to reward their employees in a non-taxable form by giving them non-cash benefits, but as employers realised this was a cost effective way of paying people, the Inland Revenue brought in new rules to make virtually all benefits taxable. Over the years employers have found imaginative ways to avoid the tax system, but it is fair to say that most of these gaps in the legislation have now been closed, and it is extremely difficult for an employee to receive something that is not subject to tax.

Employers are instructed to deduct tax under PAYE at the time a payment is made and to declare expenses and benefits on Form P11D at each year end. This means that if the Inland Revenue or the (Department of Social Security (DSS) find out that certain amounts or benefits have not been notified, so that no tax or NI has been paid, it is usually the employer who foots the bill for any unpaid deductions. For large employers an Inland Revenue investigation into their PAYE system ranging back over a number of years can give rise to demands for unpaid tax and NI in seven figures!

The 1989 Finance Act contains revised penalties for employers, including a maximum penalty of £3000 for each Form P11D wrongly completed. Employers who become wary about sending forms in, in case they are wrong, are in no better position, because the Finance Act contains revised penalties for late returns, some of which are automatic.

In the sophisticated world of employee remuneration packages, where the current trend is for a 'cafeteria' system, whereby employees choose from a range of benefits available, great care should be taken to examine the tax and NI consequences both to the employer and the employee in these packages. Employers with a small work-force should be wary about devising their own scheme for employee benefits, as it is likely that these will fall foul of the system. It is simpler to pay employees in cash (or cheque or bank transfer), unless an employer is prepared to look closely at these special rules for benefits in kind.

It is worth mentioning at this point that the benefit legislation includes not only your employees, but also members of their family or household, so that tax cannot be avoided by, for example, paying the school fees for your employees' children. It is, however, possible to avoid NI contributions on benefits in kind, provided that they are dealt with correctly (see Chapter 8 for more information on this).

There are many instances where expenses are paid to employees in the course of their work and no benefit or 'profit element' is received by the employees. These expenses still have to be shown on Form P11D at the end of each year, and although the tax office *can* assess each employee for tax on these, they would allow a deduction equal in amount to the expense that the employee had actually paid out in connection with work. For some companies the total amount of travelling and subsistence expenses can run into thousands of pounds every year, thus generating a large amount of record-keeping and form-filling at the end of each tax year. Where the Inland Revenue can agree that there is no tax liability arising on these payments, because they are a pure reimbursement of actual business expenses, they may then grant employers dispensations, which means that returns of the specified expenses do not have to be made at the year end. (More details of this sytem are given in Chapter 4.)

Married women

There are no special rules for employers in operating PAYE for married women. They are employees in the same way as any other individual and entitled to tax-free pay notified to you by way of a code from the tax office. The tax regime for married people is in the process of change, but this is unlikely to affect the method of PAYE calculations by employers.

National Insurance for married women may in some circumstances vary from the standard categories, and great care should be taken in this area as under-deductions are usually made good by the employer. (There is more on this topic in Chapter 7.)

It is, of course, this section of the population who are most likely to claim Statutory Maternity Pay (SMP) (see Chapter 11 for most information).

Under 16s

Employers have long since stopped sending children up chimneys with flue brushes, but there are many young people employed throughout the UK, for example as paperboys and girls. The PAYE system covers individuals who are employees, and there is no age limit whatsoever. You are liable to income tax from the day you are born until the day you die if you earn over the permitted amount, and to a certain extent even after that! National Insurance contributions do not start until an employee reaches the age of 16, but there is no such limit for income tax. It is pretty clear to any employer that paperboys and girls will be attending school and their earnings in the year will not exceed the taxable limit. It is, however, difficult to prove conclusively to an Inland Revenue audit team that these employees are school children. There have been instances where unpaid tax has been sought by the Revenue because the PAYE procedures have not been followed correctly. It is therefore advisable to follow the rules for casual employees or part-timers (detailed earlier in this chapter) to avoid any such complications.

4
Types of Payments and Deductions

The basic rule for employers is that payments made to employees, whether in cash or benefit in kind, as a reward for their services, are taxable. There are few exceptions to this rule. If a payment is made in cash as a reward for services, then tax should be deducted under the Pay As You Earn (PAYE) system. If a reward is made by a benefit in kind in some way, then notification is usually required on Form P11D (return of expenses payments and benefits for directors and certain employees) or Form P9D (for other employees) at the end of each tax year. There are only a handful of small concessions where payments are not taxable (for example, 15p per day luncheon vouchers) and these are instanced in this chapter.

Employers should be in no doubt that standard payments of wages or salary, whether weekly or monthly or some other interval, are taxed at the time of payment under PAYE. It is the purpose of this chapter to discuss the other payment and deduction situations that employers may have to deal with and at least should know about.

Overtime, bonus and commission

One of the features common to all three of these payments is that they are likely to be paid some time after they have been earned. For example, the overtime for one week will be paid with the wages for the following week. The PAYE system does not require employers to do any complicated reworking of the previous week's figures to put in the amount of overtime earned in that week. PAYE is based on when a payment is made, so that it is quite in order for an employer to add together the wages for the current week and overtime, etc for a previous period, and deduct tax in the week in which the payment is made. If, however, payment of a bonus is delayed, then tax deductions are due to be made at the time the employee becomes entitled to the money.

In the case of an employee who regularly pays tax each week or month

35

on his basic wage or salary, it can appear that any payment for bonus or overtime seems to be heavily taxed. Employees sometimes see this as a disincentive to earn extra money. This is because the tax-free pay which each employee is allowed to earn is spread evenly over the year and the employee will have received the benefit of this tax-free portion of his pay against his normal earnings for the week or month. Any additional payments are then wholly taxed without benefit of a tax-free portion, so that the percentage of tax paid on the additional payment is higher than the tax paid on the regular payment.

This situation can be made much worse in the early months of the tax year where large amounts of bonus may be due for the previous year. The tax system allows an employee to pay tax at the basic rate on a set figure of income before tax is then paid at a higher rate. The tax tables apportion the 'basic rate band' over each tax week or month, so that over a whole year a higher-rate taxpayer pays the increased amount from the beginning of the year and not just towards the end of the year as his total income exceeds that basic rate band. Because of this, the tax tables are designed to assume that the rate of pay in week 1 will continue throughout the year. The tables do not take into account the fact that the week 1 payment may be greatly increased because of an annual bonus. Where an employee suffers deductions at the higher rate of tax because of this, and his income falls to its normal rate in the following weeks, then the tax paid is evened out, so that any higher-rate tax deducted will be refunded over the following weeks.

An employer is sometimes tempted not to deduct tax at the higher rates from an employee in these circumstances, but instead assume that the employee will stay in the employment long enough for his average rate of pay to fall back within the basic rate band. It is not, however, uncommon for an employee to leave a job after that annual bonus is paid, and if the employer has not correctly used the tax tables and deductions to include the higher rate of tax, then the pay and tax figures on Form P45 will not agree with the tax tables. In some instances the employer may be asked not only to explain the discrepancy, but also to account for the tax underpaid.

Holiday pay

Nowadays the majority of employees are employed under contracts of employment which entitle them to a certain number of weeks paid holiday in a year. Holiday pay is part of employees' reward for working for the rest of the year, and it is therefore taxable.

The UK has a history of paying employees on a weekly basis, and this makes the system of holiday pay more complicated, both for tax and

National Insurance (NI) purposes. If an employer has any choice in the matter, he is well advised to pay employees monthly, not simply to avoid holiday pay calculations, but so that the time-consuming task of operating PAYE is limited to 12 occasions in the year, instead of 52. Monthly paid staff are simply paid one-twelfth of their annual salary each pay day, so if any holiday is taken during a month this will make no difference to the amount of payment or the PAYE calculations, unless for some reason they are paid a different rate of pay for holiday periods.

Staff who are paid at weekly intervals will normally ask to have their pay for the weeks when they will be on holiday paid to them with the pay for their last week at work. This means that, say, three weeks' pay is paid on the same day. Under the normal PAYE rules one week's proportion of the annual free pay will be allowed against three weeks' money, so that heavy deductions of tax would be made that week. When the employee returns after the holiday and receives a week's money for the first week back at work, then he would have not only tax-free pay for that week, but also for the two holiday weeks, and would pay less than normal tax.

There are employers who insist on operating this system for their employees but employers are allowed to give employees the credit for the tax-free pay they would have been entitled to if the holiday weeks were normal weeks paid at the right time. This means that an employer can advance the tax week for calculations of holiday pay. For example, for an employee going on two weeks holiday at week 17 of the tax year, the employer may add together the week's pay for a working week, two weeks' holiday pay, and work out the tax as if the three weeks were going to be paid in tax week 19. When the employee returns to work he is paid as normal in tax week 20.

There are occasions when employees do not return to work after a holiday, and in this case the employer will have to decide when the contract of employment was terminated. Employees in this situation will often say that they finished work for the employer on the Friday that they last worked, and it is often advisable for the employer to treat this as the date of leaving the employment. In this case, the date of leaving given on Form P45 will not tally with the last week number for which PAYE was operated. In this instance a note on Form P45 to the effect that holiday pay was paid in advance, but the employee did not return to work, should be sufficient explanation.

Where an employee notifies you before he goes on holiday that he is actually resigning from his job, or where you are paying accrued holiday pay to an employee who has given notice, you need not advance the tax week to the end of the holiday pay period. Where you know that an employee will not return to work with you, simply add together all payments due to that employee whether holiday pay, overtime, etc, and tax them in the tax week in which the last date of payment falls, normally the last date of work.

The rules for NIC on weekly holiday pay are more complicated even than tax deductions, and constitute a further pointer – if one were needed – towards monthly pay. (See Chapter 8 for further discussion of this.)

Sick pay and Statutory Sick Pay (SSP)

Employers often have occupational sick-pay schemes for employees, so that normal wages or salary payments are kept up even though the employee may be absent from work because of sickness. Larger employers will have an occupational sick-pay scheme which sets out rules for notifications of sickness, which will include requirements for medical certificates, and the length of time for which full pay or reduced pay will be paid. Payments under any occupational sick-pay scheme, whether paid formally or informally, are payments under the contract of employment and are fully taxable under PAYE in the normal way. The payment of SSP is also subject to PAYE deductions. (See Chapter 10 for more details.)

Maternity pay and Statutory Maternity Pay (SMP)

Many employers have an occupational maternity pay scheme in addition to their occupational sick-pay scheme. Any payments of occupational maternity pay made by an employer are subject to tax under PAYE as if they were wages or salary.

SMP was introduced on 6 April 1987 and is similar in some ways to SSP. As with SSP, all amounts paid to the employee under SMP are taxable and deductions should be made in exactly the same way as for pay. (See Chapter 11 for further details on SMP.)

Luncheon vouchers and payments for meals

An employee who spends money on lunch or another meal is normally seen to be incurring a 'living expense' as opposed to a 'business expense'. This means that, under the normal rules, if you give employees an allowance for food, it counts as a taxable reward of the employment.

There is a special concession in the case of luncheon vouchers and these can be given to employees tax-free provided that:

1. They are used only for meals and cannot be transferred.

2. If they are supplied to part of the work-force only, they are made available to lower-paid staff in preference to higher-paid staff.
3. Their value does not exceed 15p per day.

If you consider 15p per day insufficient to provide your employees with a lunch, you are at liberty to increase this amount, but any excess over 15p per day is taxable under PAYE.

It is possible for an employer to provide a heavily subsidised staff restaurant at no tax liability to employees, provided that the facilities are available for all the staff to use and not, for instance, just for directors. This could mean that employees benefit at a rate far in excess of the tax concessions for luncheon vouchers where the amount (free of tax) is currently 15p per day. This is a clear anomaly of the PAYE system, and many employers, where they have the facilities, do provide subsidised restaurants for their employees, who receive what is, in effect, a tax-free benefit.

Different rules apply to employees who are sent away from their normal place of employment, which loses them the opportunity to take lunch at the subsidised staff restaurant. Where an employee incurs an extra cost to himself because he is working away from his normal place of employment then a tax-free reimbursement may be made to him for the cost of the lunch (or any other meal) which has been purchased. The employee will normally make a claim for this expense supported by a voucher (or receipt) for the meal he has bought. If a tightly controlled system for reimbursements has been introduced, such expenses may be paid free of tax or NI liability under PAYE.

Employers faced with a large number of such expense claims from employees are tempted to fix a standard rate of allowance so that employees can claim this without providing a supporting voucher. These payments are often called subsistence payments or allowances. They may also be termed 'round sum allowances', and both the Inland Revenue and the DSS take the view that these should be liable for tax and NI deductions under PAYE, as there is no evidence to support the claim that the amounts have actually been spent. For tax purposes only, it is possible to obtain a dispensation for such payments where it can be shown that the amounts do no more than recompense the employee for the expenditure which he has incurred. The DSS, however, do not have a dispensation system and it could be that employers may not be required to deduct tax from a payment, but still have an obligation to deduct NI (see Chapter 8).

Certainly, the easiest way for employers to avoid such complications is simply to reimburse actual expenses incurred by employees in the course of their work.

Profit-related pay

An employer may decide to link part of the pay of a group of employees to the profits which the firm makes, and where this is done within specified guidelines there is a tax advantage to those employees. This tax advantage allows for half of the profit-related pay up to a specified figure, currently £3000, to be paid without tax deductions. The initial rules of the scheme were so complicated that fewer than 1000 employers applied in the first year. There has been some relaxation of the rules and this may encourage more employers to participate. Full details of the scheme can be obtained from:

The Profit-Related Pay Office,
St Mungo's Road,
Cumbernauld,
Glasgow G67 1YZ
(Tel 0236 736121).

Gift vouchers and Christmas boxes

When is a gift not a gift? – that is the question.

When one individual gives something to another individual in recognition of his personal qualities, that is in no way related to the recipient's employment, then that gift may well escape taxation under the PAYE rules. There is, however, all the difference in the world between a gift on a twenty-first birthday from an employer with a small business employing three people who all work together daily, and a gift on marriage from an employer with 50,000 employees, where the personnel officer authorising the gift may never have met the recipient. In the latter instance the Inland Revenue may well take the view that the gift is a reward for services of the employment and is therefore taxable. If an employer feels that he can convince his local tax office that what he has made is a personal gift, then the employer is free to choose not to operate PAYE on a cash amount, or enter the benefit on Form P11D at the end of the year.

The Inland Revenue are quite specific in their instructions to employers regarding Christmas boxes, vouchers and hampers, etc. If the Christmas box is in cash, or a voucher of some kind that can be exchanged for cash, then the whole of the amount should be included in pay, and tax deducted in the normal way. If the Christmas box is in the form of goods, eg a food hamper or a voucher that can only be exchanged for goods, then full details of the cost to the employer should be entered on the end-of-year returns, Forms P9D or P11D (see Chapter 15 for more details).

Prize incentive schemes

It is a popular practice today for employers to reward their employees for extra effort at work by way of an incentive scheme, whereby employees receive items such as hi-fi equipment, personal computers or holidays. These all form part of a reward for the services of the employment and are therefore taxable, whether the employee is given the goods purchased by the employer, or a voucher exchangable for those goods. Full details of the cost to the employer should always be entered on Form P9D or P11D at the end of each year, so that the employee can pay tax on them. This is often considered to be an unfair burden on employees who have received a television set, for example, and are then asked to pay tax when they have actually received no money. If the employer wishes he may set up a 'taxed award scheme' with the Inland Revenue, and pay to the Inland Revenue after the end of each year the basic rate tax, on the grossed up value of course, on behalf of those employees concerned.

This system of payment can also be used by third parties. This means that where a manufacturer of goods rewards the sales force of a distributing company who are not his employees, the manufacturer can pay to the Inland Revenue the basic rate tax on any awards that he makes.

Long-service awards

It is still possible to give long-serving members of staff a gold watch or clock on retirement without having to incur an income tax charge. There are, however, as in all things fiscal, strict rules to be observed. A long-service award in a tangible form, eg a watch, may be made tax-free provided the following conditions are met:

1. The period of service with the company is for not less than 20 years.
2. No similar award has been made to that person within the previous 10 years.
3. The cost to the employer does not (currently) exceed £20 per year of service.

Staff suggestion schemes

A further Inland Revenue concession operates in this area, whereby awards are made to staff in recognition of suggestions they make to improve working practices which benefit the company.

Again there are precise rules to be followed if awards are to be made tax-free. These are as follows:

1. There must be a formally constituted scheme open to all employees on equal terms.
2. The suggestion should be outside the scope of the employee's normal duties. (This means that if it is part of an employee's job to be innovative, then no separate award under a suggestion scheme can be made to him for such a suggestion.)
3. Awards have to be made, following the implementation of the suggestion, directly to the employee concerned.
4. The award is related to the improvement in efficiency or cost saving achieved by the suggestion.
5. The maximum tax-free award is the lesser of £5000 or 50 per cent of the financial benefit to the firm during the first year of implementation or 10 per cent of the financial benefit over a five-year period.
6. It is possible to award £25 to employees under such a scheme for 'meritorious effort', even where the suggestion is not implemented.

Tool allowances

Where an employee comes to work and uses the employer's tools and machinery to carry out his job, there is no tax charge on the employee for the use of that machinery! There may well, however, be a tax charge where the employee takes the employer's tools home and uses them for his own purposes (see Chapter 15). If an employee has to provide his own tools and equipment and the employer makes an allowance to him each year towards the cost of these tools, then the cash paid should be added to pay for PAYE purposes in the normal way.

Some allowance can be made for tools which an employee buys in order to carry out his job. He is able to claim on his own tax return for money he spends wholly exclusively and necessarily in the performance of the duties of his employment. In practice many employees do not make such a claim either through ignorance, or because they suspect that the rules for deductions from employment income are so carefully worded that it is almost impossible to get any relief. In particular, if any private use is made of the tools then the use is not exclusively for business and no deduction can be made. Many large trade unions in the building or engineering trades have agreed with the Inland Revenue over the years for certain standard tool allowances to be given to their members. It is possible therefore for many tradesmen to obtain an allowance against their own tax bills without having to produce itemised vouchers each year.

Tips and service charges

The Inland Revenue regard a tip or gratuity as part of the reward an employee receives for performing the duties of his job. This means that it is fully taxable, and the fact that a person other than the employer gives the employee the tip is irrelevant. Difficulty arises when tax is to be collected on these gratuities and the employer is unable to do this because, for example, the money does not pass through his hands.

The normal procedure for employees such as hairdressers, where the customer gives a tip directly to the employee, is that the tax office will estimate the amount of tips receivable in a year and make an adjustment in the employee's code by reducing his personal allowances, so that tax is, in effect, paid on the tips throughout the year. This method of taxing tips does not involve the employer at all.

Complications arise where the employer has a scheme for tips whereby they are all collected and distributed by him. Once the employer assumes control of the collection and distribution of the money then he must add it to gross pay and operate PAYE in the normal way.

In some large hotels it is customary for the head waiter to collect and distribute the tips to the remainder of the employees and in this case he has to operate PAYE on the tips he pays out. This is known as the 'tronc' system and the head waiter would be called the tronc master. The tronc master makes returns to the Inland Revenue at the end of the year.

Travelling and subsistence expenses

There can be few businesses today that have never had to make payments to employees for travel required in the course of work. Such payments may range from those made to an international sales executive incurring flights and hotel bills around the world amounting to thousands of pounds every year, to the employee in a small shop who is asked to make an urgent delivery to a customer by taxi or even on the local bus.

The whole area of employee expenses has received increasing attention from both the Inland Revenue and the DSS recently, because in many cases both departments are seeking PAYE deductions in areas where previously they have turned a blind eye.

The Inland Revenue and the DSS are highlighting 'profit elements' of travelling and subsistence payments, and clearly, if the employee profits from the expense, then that profit is a taxable part of his pay. If an employee is paid 20p per mile for driving his own car on company business there is unlikely to be any profit in this for him. However, if the sum paid were £1 per mile then most people would see that the employee was making a profit on the scheme. There are now many employees receiving expenses, therefore it is worthwhile for the government departments to pursue their share, which when added together can be around 45 per cent of that profit.

The prospect of a DSS investigator totalling up all the mileage allowances paid in a year for a large employer, and asking for a percentage of the profit element, say 4p or 5p a mile, can be frightening, particularly when the arithmetic comes out into hundreds of thousands of pounds. Many employers are trying to consider ways of avoiding what is for them a growing problem.

There is one certain way to avoid the complications of tax and NI on expenses payments, and this is to simply reimburse employees for the actual expenses they incur in the performance of their duties. This means that employees will come back to the office with hotel bills, train ticket receipts, bus tickets, etc, and claim a reimbursement exactly equal to the amount they have spent. Where this is done the Inland Revenue and the DSS accept that, provided the expenses are incurred for a business purpose, there is no tax and NI to be paid. This method also enables the employer to retain the receipts, which will often include Value Added Tax (VAT), and will enable him to claim the appropriate VAT deduction.

The only problem with a pure reimbursement system is that it is difficult to quantify exactly the amount of expense an employee will incur in driving his own car on company business. Here again there is a simple way to avoid the problem and this is to pay a mileage rate which contains no profit element to the employee, so that no tax or NI contributions will be due. The DSS have now agreed that where the standard Automobile Association (AA) and Royal Automobile Club (RAC) mileage rates are paid to employees for business miles, then no NI is due from the employee or the employer. The Inland Revenue have now accepted that there is no profit element to the employee in AA and RAC mileage rates and have issued letters to employers identifying the mileage rates they would consider to be profit-free. The mileage rates paid should reflect the size of the car's engine, and if possible the total mileage travelled in a year, so that it may be necessary to pay a range of mileage allowances. The advice to employers is now quite clear: pay a simple mileage rate below the AA or RAC rates and avoid any tax or NIC complications.

Many employers operate a system whereby each month a round sum is paid to employees who have to use their cars on company business, so that a standard amount for example £50 per month, is paid in addition to a reduced rate per mile, for example 15p. This may have the same net effect as the calculations using mileage rates as mentioned above, but does not have the same effect for tax or NI. The NI complications are detailed in Chapter 8 and for tax purposes the £50 per month is considered to be a 'round sum allowance' and round sum allowances are to be subjected to tax under PAYE as pay. This method is therefore not recommended for employers who wish to avoid tax and NI complications.

Relocation expenses are usually reimbursed to employees moving house because of their job. It is possible to agree with your tax office the items and levels of expenses that can be paid tax free.

Round sum allowances

Round sum allowances for any expense are fraught with difficulties and should be avoided if at all possible. Employers with large numbers of staff may have an Inland Revenue dispensation for expenses (details given below), so that, in effect, a round sum or standard amount can be paid to employees for certain items of expenditure without incurring a tax charge. The Inland Revenue may, for example, agree that a daily subsistence rate of, say, £5 may be paid to employees who are required to work away from the office and incur small amounts of expenditure. Inland Revenue dispensations would not normally be given for large amounts of round sum allowances. Chapter 8, dealing with the NI on expenses should be read in this context, as the DSS have no dispensation procedure whatsoever, so that a dispensation for tax is not effective in any way for NI.

Difficulties have arisen in recent years following PAYE inspections where employers have been asked to repay to the Inland Revenue and the DSS large amounts of unpaid tax and NI on many items of expenses previously thought tax- and NI-free. If you think that your employees profit from an expense payment that you make to them, then you should be operating PAYE on that profit.

Historically, payments of expenses have been made to employees not through payroll, but through a petty cash system handled by the cashier or accounts department. Cashiers or accountants do not normally operate PAYE on anything they pay and are often unaware of the new stance taken by the government departments regarding profit elements. The trend nowadays, particularly for those companies already taken to task by a PAYE audit team, is to pay all sums to employees, including expenses, through payroll. This means that the opportunity is readily available for employers to deduct tax and NI from relevant items at the time of payment. (For NI purposes the employer to a great extent loses his right to deduct NI contributions if he does not do this in the earnings period in which the amount is paid to the employees.)

The message is clear to employers: they need a properly controlled and vouched expense system, where employees' expenses are authorised by superiors, and any payments, where possible, are made through the payroll system. If these simple rules were followed employers would not be in the position of having to settle demands for tax and NI. There are two main reasons why employers do not do this: (1) the administrative burden involved; and (2) the desire to reward employees by avoiding their tax and NI contributions.

Dispensations

You will see from the section on travelling and subsistence expenses that employers really do need a properly controlled and fully vouched expenses system to satisfy the stringent requirements of the Inland Revenue (and the DSS – see Chapter 8). This is because if either department can show that any part of an expense payment made to an employee is a 'profit' of the employment that has not been paid out in doing the job, then usually the employer will foot the bill for any unpaid tax and NI contributions.

When you have gone to the time and trouble of setting up a well-documented and fully-vouched expense system you will have a considerable amount of paperwork on your hands each year, which has still to be itemised and totalled up and reported to the Revenue on Forms P11D for each of the employees in that category. There is, however, light at the end of this tunnel. You will be able to show the Tax Inspector that your expense systems are so well controlled that there is no profit element to employees, that there is therefore no tax lost to the Inland Revenue, and you will then be able to apply for a 'dispensation' for all those expense and subsistence payments. The Tax Inspector dealing with you as an employer, when he has satisfied himself regarding your expense system and the employees covered by it, can issue an employer with a formal statement of dispensation, detailing the types of expenses and the employees covered and the date from which the dispensation starts. The good news is that for all expenses covered by the dispensation, no return need be made at the end of the year on form P11D. The object of this is to save both employers and the Inland Revenue a great deal of work in the preparation and examination of these returns.

The Inland Revenue actively encourage employers to apply for a dispensation for expenses but such an application can carry a 'government health warning'. The tax authorities need to satisfy themselves about your expense systems, and employers have found that in order to do this they have paid an audit inspection type visit which has unearthed undisclosed items, giving rise to a tax bill. Employers are therefore well advised not to apply for a dispensation until they can be assured that there are no lurking liabilities for tax and NI. It is becoming popular for employers to have a 'health check' carried out by their own accountants, or a firm of accountants, who specialise in this kind of work.

Once a dispensation has been granted to an employer the terms of the dispensation must be complied with, or it becomes invalid. This means that if a dispensation is granted for a mileage rate of, say, 25p per mile and some years later the company chooses to increase this to 30p per mile, the dispensation does not apply to the revised amount. It is, of course, possible to refer back to the Tax Inspector for a revision of the dispensation, and it is a good idea to review the document at, say, yearly intervals, to ensure that it is up to date.

Payments on cessation of employment

Payments on cessation of employment, which include compensation for loss of office, golden handshakes, payments in lieu of notice, *ex gratia* payments, etc, all have one thing in common: they are paid after the contract of employment has come to an end. Many employers for this reason think that all these payments automatically escape taxation but this is not the case. If the payment arises out of the employment, and is a reward for the services of that employment then it is taxable in the normal way. This means that simple payments of bonus, paid after someone has left the employment, do not escape the normal tax rules. There are, however, very complicated rules for payments that are not part of normal salary.

Before looking at these special rules, there are clear circumstances in which payments are fully taxable, the first being where the employee has a contractual right to receive the payment. This will often arise in the case of payment in lieu of notice, where the contract of employment contains a 'break' clause. Such a clause is commonly found in the kind of industry where on resignation an employee is escorted off the premises forthwith because of the sensitive nature of his work. This situation may be specifically included in such contracts, which include words to the effect that if the employee is made to leave the premises as soon as notice is given, then he will be paid the three months' notice money for the period of notice. This gives the employee a contractual right to receive that money and he is liable to be taxed on it without concession.

An employee who, for some disciplinary or other reason, is given notice by his employer and asked to leave immediately, is entitled to pay in lieu of notice in respect of the amount of notice period he is entitled to under the terms of the contract of employment. In this case the money he receives is not pay at all, but is strictly liquidated damages for the loss suffered in the breaking of the contract. He has no contractual right to this sum of money and this payment is normally wholly tax-free. There is a concession on payments which fall outside the normal PAYE system, and this limits the tax-free amount to £30,000. This is normally sufficient to cover any standard amount of pay in lieu of notice.

The term '*ex gratia*' payment is widely misused because in essence it means something for nothing. The government departments take the view that modern companies are unlikely to give a past employee money for nothing in return, and like to argue that such payments are in fact a reward for past services. In order to qualify as an *ex gratia* payment, a sum of money to a past employee must be in respect of his personal qualities, as opposed to being in respect of the work he may have done for the company for the last 30 years or whatever. Employers should always be careful therefore when paying such amounts of money to make sure that any letters or other documentation relating to such a payment does not in any way indicate that the payment is a reward for past services.

Having considered carefully the circumstances in which an employer is making such a payment on termination of employment, he may properly consider that the first £30,000 is exempt from tax under the special rules, but there is a further pitfall. If an employer habitually makes these payments, and employees get to know that when they leave or retire they are likely to receive a lump sum payment, then the expectation of the sum of money by the employees is sufficient for the Inspector of Taxes to consider the whole of the amount taxable. Where a firm is in the process of making a number of staff redundant, and wants to put together a reasonable package in addition to any sum payable under the statutory redundancy scheme, then it is worthwhile seeking professional advice on drawing up a scheme, so that it does not fall foul of the special rules. Where payments under such a scheme are considered to be a genuine redundancy and follow certain guidelines, the Inland Revenue will accept that they are not taxable, even though employees may have an expectation of a sum of money.

This whole area of payments after an employee has left is very complicated and is one in which the Inland Revenue take a considerable interest. Most instances of payments go by unnoticed, but large sums tend to make headlines, for instance, where the recipient is a celebrity in the football world. Payments over £30,000 should only be made after considering the complex rules, and preferably after taking professional advice. This is particularly the case where staff changes are to be made at about the time of a company re-organisation or take-over, as the timing of the payments may affect the corporation tax that the company pays.

Pensions

Pensioners are, of course, taxable, as detailed in Chapter 3, so that any payment of pension by an employer or indeed a pension fund, is treated as pay and taxed in the normal way. At the time of retirement there are great changes in an individual's circumstances for income tax and these often result in the wrong deductions being made sometimes for months. Because of this, correspondence from both the pensioner and the tax district need to be dealt with promptly, particularly in those first few months. Subsequent years of pension payments tend to be less complicated than for a normal employee.

Deductions from pay

Both income tax and NI are deductions from pay, and are calculated on the taxable pay and pay subject to NI respectively, which is not necessarily the same figure. Employers should not be tempted to compute either of these statutory deductions on the net result of having deducted either of them from gross pay first!

Superannuation or pension contributions

There has been a growth industry in personal pensions over the last few years, so that employees are more easily able to make their own pension arrangements. Employers with pension schemes need to ensure a flow of money into their own funds, and have found new ways to encourage employees to join their in-house schemes.

There is a concession for income tax that contributions to an approved pension fund may be deducted from gross pay before tax is calculated. In order to obtain approval for the scheme the employer must satisfy the Superannuation Funds Office of the Inland Revenue that his scheme does provide a certain level of benefit on retirement, and the insurance companies who commonly market pension schemes will handle all this for an employer (there is no similar concession for NI – see Chapter 8).

Give as you earn

A new concession for income tax has recently been introduced whereby employees may contribute money to a charity or charities of their choice, have the deductions made through payroll, and obtain tax relief on the donation up to a set limit. The limit is £240 per year (previously £120) and this, of course, can be paid at amounts up to £20 per month or the weekly equivalent. For tax relief to be obtained by employees the employer has to make the proper arrangements and should contact his local tax office about setting up a scheme.

5

Starters, Leavers and People-related Events

Payroll would be a much simpler operation if employees started in your employment on the date they left school and stayed with you until the date they retired. This, of course, is rarely the case. During a tax year you will normally have to deal with people who start and stop working for you for a variety of reasons: because they are on strike, on maternity leave, or even because they die.

A payroll system has to be able to cope with all these eventualities, but the most common is the ordinary run-of-the-mill starter or leaver.

New employees

Employers often try to fit new employees into a variety of categories, including full-time, part-time, casual, Saturday morning, seasonal or holiday only. It can be confusing to try and adapt the Pay As You Earn (PAYE) system to cover such a wide range of categories of workers. In reality, for PAYE, there are two kinds of employee: those who bring Form P45 and those who do not. Form P45 is the leaving certificate given to an employee by his last employer, so normally people who have been in employment before joining your company should have been given Form P45 and be able to bring it with them. There are a number of circumstances in which previously employed people do not bring a P45: they may have lost it or the old employer has not yet prepared it but the lack of this form should not affect your standard procedures.

If the new employee hands you Form P45 parts II and III (part I will have been sent to the tax office by the previous employer) then you should fill in all the items on part III of the form and send this to your local tax office. Tax offices today have very little communication with employees so it does assist them if as much information as possible can be put on this form, including the employee's address. You should keep part II of the form for your own records, and the tax office require that these are kept for at least three years after the end of the tax year in which the employee left your company.

The P45 should be examined to check that it is for the current tax year and then the pay and tax deducted should be checked against the tax tables for the week or month shown on the form. If the tax-deducted figure does not agree with the tax tables, you should use the tax-table figure, and enter this in the box at the bottom of part III of the form. The tax office will then check with the previous employer to see why the figures are incorrect.

If Form P45 is for the last tax year and the employee starts with you before 26 April you may use the code on the form. If, however, the form is for the last tax year and you take the employee on after 26 April, use the current emergency code with nil previous pay and tax details. If the P45 is older than this then simply use the emergency code.

The second category of employee is those who do not have Form P45. You should then consider whether the employee is going to work for you for more than one week, or for one week or less and, refer to the tables A and B at paragraph D43 in the Inland Revenue's booklet *Employer's Guide to PAYE*.

These flow charts are reproduced here as Figures 5.1 and 5.2 and you should try to comply with the directions given in all cases. Employees with no P45 should be handed Form P46 and asked to sign it. This form asks the employee to sign either a certificate to say that he or she is a school-leaver and has not been drawing unemployment benefit (in which case you can use the emergency code on the cumulative basis), or the certificate which declares that it is the employee's only or main job, in which case you may use the emergency code on a week 1/month 1 basis. In any other circumstance, where either the employee does not return Form P46 to you or does not sign either of the certificates, then you should deduct tax using the basic rate (BR) table and not the emergency code.

Many employers are still assuming that employees without P45s should have the emergency code operated against their pay, but this is not always appropriate. The system changed on 6 April 1982, and since then employers have been instructed to deduct tax at the basic rate, so catching any employees who may be in the 'Black Economy'. The situation is slightly different for an employee who is going to work for you for one week or less, and in this case you do not have to give the employee a P46. You may use the emergency code on a week 1 or month 1 basis unless you know the employee has another job, in which case you must deduct tax using code BR.

The instructions regarding new employees are quite clear, and employers should try to comply with them in all circumstances. This is one of the areas most likely to be discovered in the event of a PAYE audit and

Table A

► prepare form P46

► find out the employee's NI number — leaflet NP15 tells you how to do this

► ask the employee to consider either Certificate A or B on the front of form P46 and sign one of the certificates if appropriate

► issue coding claim form P15 (where the chart below tells you to) and a reply envelope. Fill in the employee's NI number in the box provided in Section A of the form and also complete the tax reference box. Employers dealt with at Centre 1 can ignore the tax reference box.

► follow the chart below

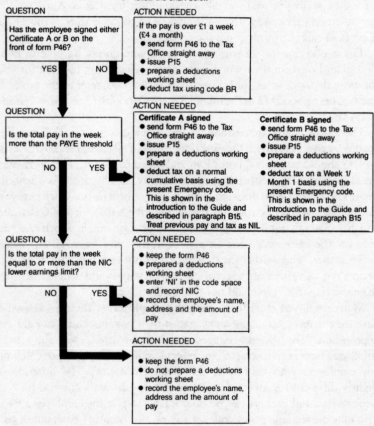

Figure 5.1 *Employee working for more than one week*

Source: Inland Revenue, p7

Table B

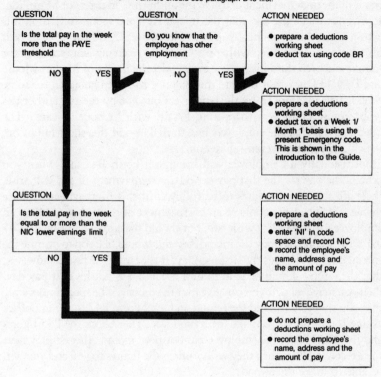

Figure 5.2 *Employee working one week or less*

Source: Inland Revenue, p7

the Inland Revenue take the view that without Form P46 from your employee, then the job with you was his second job and you should have stopped income tax at the basic rate. The Inland Revenue will simply ask you for all the basic rate income tax for all such employees going back over the last six years. There are employers for whom this calculation would result in the underpayment of tax to the authorities in excess of £1 million. It was not that long ago that the Inland Revenue successfully took this action against national newspapers in Fleet Street. Falsification of records by employees was rife, with print-workers receiving untaxed pay for second and even third jobs, some even under the names of Mickey Mouse and Donald Duck. But because this practice had been going on for some time it was overlooked by the employers but not by the tax authorities who require employers to operate PAYE with 'reasonable care'. The outcome was that the employers had to make good this short-fall of tax which amounted to seven-figure numbers.

Occasionally an employee will bring you Form P45 and when you process the pay for the first pay period an overpayment of tax will arise, there are special procedures to be followed if this overpayment is more than £100. The rules apply to an overpayment of more than £100 on an employee's first pay-day with you, but should the employee bring his P45 in for the second pay-day the Inland Revenue would like you to operate the special rules as if it was the first pay-day. If the employee insists, however, that the refund should be paid to him because it is not his first pay-day, then you may feel that you can give him the money. The special rules state that you should withhold the refund and send Form P47 to the tax office asking for authority to make the refund due. They check the P45 figures and if satisfied that the employee has not been in any other employment since receiving P45, then they will confirm the figures to you and you will be able to make the refund.

Leavers

The first thing an employer should do when an employee leaves his employment, is to make sure that he stops paying him. It is not uncommon for a personnel department to deal with the formal notification of an employee leaving and for the information not to get passed to the payroll department, who continues to pay the person after he has left. With payments commonly made by bank transfer this is particularly easy, since the payroll will always be processed before the pay date. (The success of a payroll department can be measured in how effective its lines of communication are with other departments in the company, particularly personnel. It follows that good payroll people are normally good communicators.)

When an employee leaves, the payroll office could by standard procedure let him know that his normal salary will be received on the last working day, and any payments of overtime, bonus, etc by cheque the next week. Mistakes are very often made by payroll offices hurriedly trying to compute pay and allowances on the last working day, including any overtime, etc that would normally be paid in the following week. Provided employees receive their standard wages, they are normally happy to wait for any additional payments, provided they are notified of this. When you have made all the known payments to an employee on leaving, an employer must fill in Form P45 with as much information as possible, including the employee's last known address, and sent part I to the tax office. Parts II and III can either be given to the employee or sent on to him with his final pay cheque.

If there are amounts of money which are unknown at the date on which the P45 is being prepared, then the P45 should be prepared on the basis of information to date. Any additional payments after the P45 has been issued should be taxed at the basic rate and no further P45 prepared. The end-of-year details will include the additional payment and tax, and the final code on the end-of-year return will reflect the BR status. (See Chapter 4 for information on redundancy payments.)

The P45 is known as the leaving certificate as the employer certifies the details as being correct before he sends part I to the tax office. Because of this, employers should never be tempted to issue a duplicate certificate if, for example, the employee says he has lost the original. The employee in these circumstances should be asked to refer to the tax office.

Death of an employee

It is obvious that no further payment can be made to an employee after he has died, and any money due should be made to the personal representatives of the deceased. The personnel office of the company will normally contact the relatives to find out who are the personal representatives or the solicitors acting for the deceased. Any final payments of salary, etc should then be made either to the personal representative or the solicitors. Form P45 should be issued and all three parts sent to the tax office, a capital letter D should be entered in the box at the bottom of the form. The name and address of the personal representative or solicitors can also be shown in the employee's private address box on part I of the P45.

If the amount of money due to the estate is known or can be ascertained quickly, then the final payments should be computed and the P45 prepared, including all the pay and tax details. If there is likely to be some delay before the final payments can be computed, then P45 should be issued with a note 'further payment to be made'. If the payments made after death are made in the same tax year as previous payments, then the same tax code that was used before death should be used for the final payments. If the payments are made in the year following the year of death, then a new deductions working sheet must be used with the previous year's code on a week 1 or month 1 basis.

Strikes or trade disputes

There are special income tax provisions when employees are involved in a strike or trade dispute. Because of the normal operation of PAYE, if payroll was processed for a week when no money was paid to employees, then a refund would arise related to the amount of the employees' tax-free pay for that week. The special system in the event of a strike is to prevent the employees receiving the benefit of these tax refunds for weeks when they are not at work. There are two ways in which employers can deal with this. The first is to operate the payroll in the normal way with no pay being entered; this will give tax refunds each week, but a stop should be put to them so that they are not paid to employees. The second method is for the payroll not to be run at all until the employees return to work or the strike ends. If the strike continues over the end of a tax year, then no refunds should be made to employees, but the end-of-year certificate of pay and tax deducted can reflect the amount of refund withheld and Form P61 or P62 can be given to your employees as notification of this.

The refunds can be made to employees in the following circumstances:

1. If the employee returns to work and no longer takes part in the dispute.
2. If the employee leaves your employment altogether.
3. When the trade dispute comes to an end and employees return to work.

Part Two:
National Insurance

6
National Insurance: How It Works

Introduction

When employees are subject to Pay As You Earn (PAYE) this normally includes income tax and National Insurance (NI). These are, however, two completely separately administered systems, and employers should not be misled into thinking that NI is computed in the same way and on the same pay figures as tax.

Over the last few years employers have put forward representations that the pay figure for tax and NI should be harmonised, but the tendency seems to be in the opposite direction. In the good old days NI contributions were usually paid by employers who simply bought a stamp for each employee within the system, attaching this to a card and sent the card in once a year. In recent years NI has been earnings-related, so that the contributions can vary for each and every employee. The total contribution to be paid is usually made up of a primary and a secondary contribution, so that both employees and employers pay NI, but unfortunately not necessarily on the same amount of gross pay. This is because for employees there is a maximum amount on which NI is paid, but there is no such maximum for employers.

National Insurance is sometimes referred to as the number two tax, and indeed it has become a far more important part of the Exchequer's income over recent years. If you consider that employees pay a maximum of 9 per cent of their earnings up to a certain limit, and employers pay 10.45 per cent of earnings with no limit, then it becomes, in essence, an additional tax of nearly 20 per cent. With a basic rate of income tax of 25 per cent, this means that direct taxes can account for nearly 45 per cent of income!

There is no concept in NI comparable to the 'tax-free pay' of income tax. For tax purposes, the first band of a person's income covered by personal allowances is never subject to tax deductions, but for NI purposes, although no NI is payable up to the lower earnings level, once this level is reached then it is payable on the whole amount. Because of this difference, NI contributions are banded, so that lower amounts of earnings are charged at a lower rate of NI. The bands for some years have been set at 5 per cent, 7 per cent and then 9 per cent so that for the lower-paid the effect of NI on their pay is to some extent graduated.

The system was designed so that once a person left the 5 per cent band and his earnings attracted NI at the 7 per cent band, all the earnings were chargeable at 7 per cent. This meant that an increase of pay of £1 could result in an additional NI liability in excess of the increase in pay. To mitigate the effects of this, new bandings have been introduced from 5 October 1989, so that for employees only a 2 per cent NI rate is imposed for the first band of earnings, although the bands for employers remain at 5 per cent, 7 per cent, and 9 per cent. Although the increase in NI for employees will be from 2 per cent to 9 per cent, the effect will be lessened as the lowest band of earnings will stay at 2 per cent. This change will mean that employees and employers pay NI at different rates on earnings less than the upper earnings level from 5 October, 1989, so the NI tables will need to be used more carefully. It can no longer be assumed that the contribution will be the same for both employee and employer up to a certain level, as in the past.

To some extent NI is easier for employers to calculate than income tax. Once gross pay has been determined, then it is simply a matter of looking up that gross pay in the tables provided and copying all the figures shown on to the deductions working sheet P11. The columns in the NI contribution tables are identified in exactly the same way as they are on the deductions working sheet Form P11.

There are a number of different categories of NI, but the ones most frequently used by employers are A, B, C, D and E. Category A is the standard rate of contribution payable by employees between the ages of 16 and state pension age (65 for men, 60 for women) who are not in 'contracted-out' employment (see page 61). This means that if employers are in any doubt as to the status of an individual, or their age, then the full-rate standard category A contributions must be deducted.

Contracted-out contributions are used for employees who are members of an approved pension scheme, and the term 'contracted-out' relates to the fact that these employees have been contracted out of 'SERPS', the State Earnings-Related Pension Scheme. Where employers satisfy the Inland Revenue's Superannuation Funds Office and the Occupational Pensions Board that their pension scheme is at least as good as the government's SERPS scheme, then the employer is allowed to contract out of SERPS, and both the employer and the employees concerned pay a reduced amount of NIC.

These lower rates of contracted-out contributions are given in special NI tables, and employers should always take care that the correct tables are used for each employee. The contracted-out rates are known as categories D and E, category D being the full-rate contracted-out contribution. Whereas categories A and D are full-rate contributions, not contracted-out and contracted-out respectively, categories B and E are 'reduced-rate' contributions. These are for certain married women and widows: more detail is given in Chapter 7.

Category C contribution tables are for instances where only the employer pays NI. They are used for people over state pension age who are still in employment, or where deferment applies (see Chapter 7 for more information on both of these categories).

The NI tables are issued each year to reflect changes in NI rates or bands of earnings, and the front of each set of tables will show the tax year or period for which they are to apply. It is very easy for an employer to make a mistake, not only in the category of contribution, but also to use a set of tables for the wrong year, and because of this great care should be taken. There are limited rights of recovery of NI where the employer has deducted too little from the employee. The employer is allowed to double the employee's contribution, but only until the end of that tax year, and this may be insufficient time to make the full adjustment, particularly if the error is not discovered until March. Strictly speaking, the correct NI deductions are to be made in the same 'earnings period' as the payment of earnings is made to the employee. The totals of both employee and employer contributions are paid over to the Collector of Taxes, together with income tax at the end of each month (see Chapter 14), and full returns for each year are made and reconciled after 5 April each year (see Chapter 15).

Employers need to equip themselves with all the relevant Department of Social Security (DSS) leaflets, and the ones they need for NIC are *Yellow Book K*, *Employer's Key Leaflet Number NI268* (the most recent issue being April 1989), *Employer's Manual on National Insurance Contributions Leaflet Number NI269*, known as *Green Book 1*, and *Contribution Tables CF391*, or *Red Book 1*. In addition, *Red Book 1A* and *Red Book 1C* will be needed where the employer has a pension scheme and pays contracted-out NI. In cases of doubt or difficulties (which you will no doubt meet) there is a freephone Social Security advice line on 0800 393 539.

Earnings period

An earnings period for NI purposes is simply the interval at which earnings are normally paid. This would usually be weekly paid wages or monthly salary. If these common pay intervals are used then the appropriate NI tables for weekly or monthly earnings periods can be used. The NI contribution tables contain figures for weekly earnings at the beginning and tables of figures for monthly earnings following. Once the earnings for the week have been determined for NI purposes, then it is simply a matter of finding that figure of earnings in the weekly tables. Similarly, for monthly paid people, the monthly figure of earnings for NI purposes is found in the monthly tables. If the gross salary is between two of the amounts shown in these tables then you should use the lower of the two figures for deduction purposes.

Problems can arise when employees are paid at different intervals. These odd intervals usually fall in one of the following categories:

1. *Earnings for less than one week.* The shortest earnings period is a week, so even though employees may be paid for a few hours' or days' work, the weekly earnings tables are used. If the employee is going to work for you for the whole week, but you simply pay him on more than one occasion in the week, then you add together the earnings during that week each time payments are made and use the weekly earnings table to work out the NI due. This means that if an employee were paid £10 per day, no NI would be due for the first four days, but by the fifth day his earnings of £50 would be over the lower earnings level and NI would be due on that day.

2. *Fees per session.* Where an employee is taken on for a few hours at a time, and it is not known whether the employee will be re-employed again in the same week, then NICs are worked out on each session individually, without adding together the payments made in the same week. Employers must be quite clear about whether the employee is employed in separate sessions, or is employed for the whole week but simply on call for different hours.

3. *Intervals of more than a week.* It will often be possible, where payments are made at intervals of longer than one week, to identify a pattern to the payments. It may be that payments are in fact made every three weeks or every five weeks, or every two or three months, and where there is a regular pattern then the weekly or monthly NI tables can be used. If payments were made, for example, every three weeks, then the earnings for that period should be divided by three, looked up in the weekly NI table, and the NI contribution due multiplied by three. A similar exercise can be done for any multiples of exact weeks or months.

Where, however, the interval is not a multiple of a week or month, the exact percentage method of working out NI contributions must be used. Employers need to work out (a) how many days' earnings are being paid; (b) the lower and upper earnings limits and earnings brackets (by dividing the figures in the weekly tables by seven, and then multiplying by the number of days); (c) which rate of NI applies; and (d) how much NI is due (by multiplying the daily amount of pay by the percentage, and then the number of days worked).

4. *Payment every other week*. The payment should be divided by two, this figure looked up in the weekly contribution table and the NI due multiplied by two.

5. *Payment every other fortnight*. The payment should be divided by four, this figure looked up in the weekly contribution table and the NI due multiplied by four.

6. *Payments made at different intervals*. Employees may have a monthly salary and a quarterly bonus, or weekly wages and overtime paid monthly. In these circumstances extra payments are normally added to basic pay and NI worked out on the usual weekly or monthly earnings period. Employers should be aware that the DSS can take action where NICs are reduced because of irregular payments.

For example, where a weekly paid employee receives commission every four weeks and that amount represents a high proportion of his or her weekly pay, then the Secretary of State may direct you to use a longer earnings period and so treat all payments as if they were paid at four-weekly earnings interval. Where an employee receives a low basic wage and annual payments of commission far in excess of his annual salary, the DSS may direct that you use an annual earnings period (see below).

Annual earnings period

This special system of NI is always used for directors (see Chapter 7) and can be used for other employees where either they are paid only once in a year, or the Secretary of State has directed that an annual earnings period should be used.

Arrears of pay

NI contributions are worked out on arrears of pay when these are paid; it is not necessary to re-work all the NI contributions for the period to which the arrears relate. This is so even though the arrears may relate to a different tax year and NI rates may have changed.

Moving normal pay days

Employers will sometimes make weekly payments of wages early, for example at Christmas and bank holidays. If payments are to be made in the same tax year, then the payments are treated as if they were made on the correct day. This is the case even if two weekly payments are made together so that one is paid a week in advance: they are treated as two separate payments made on the right dates.

If a payment is moved so that it is made in a different tax year then it is the date on which payment is made that is used to find out the appropriate NI deductions. The tables for the appropriate tax year should be used. The payment should be recorded separately, so that the DSS can move the earnings if they are needed in the correct year.

Records

Because of the complexity of the modern NI system, employers should ensure that the fullest possible records are kept of earnings and deductions and any other relevant piece of information they have used in computing NI. Records of earnings and NI contributions can be shown on the deductions working sheet, Form P11, and employers will also need to keep records of correspondence with the DSS about NI numbers for new employees, or directions given by their local DSS office. The system is now so complicated that unfortunately it is possible to get different advice from a DSS local office and the head office. Therefore, it is always advisable to try to get any advice in writing, or at least to record the date of the telephone conversation and if possible the name of the DSS officer, and a note of the advice he has given you.

NI numbers

Employers must have an NI number for each employee, and if a new employee does not have his personal number, and it is not recorded on the Form P45 that is handed in to you, then you should ask the employee to obtain his NI number from his local DSS office. It is in the employee's interest to have this number because this will make sure that his contributions are credited to the correct account with the DSS. This number ensures that each employee maintains his right to a number of state benefits, including in most cases a retirement pension. There is a flow chart in *Green Book 1* which shows employers what to do in the event of employees not having an NI number. This is reproduced here as Figure 6.1.

The Inland Revenue now use NI numbers to record information for all

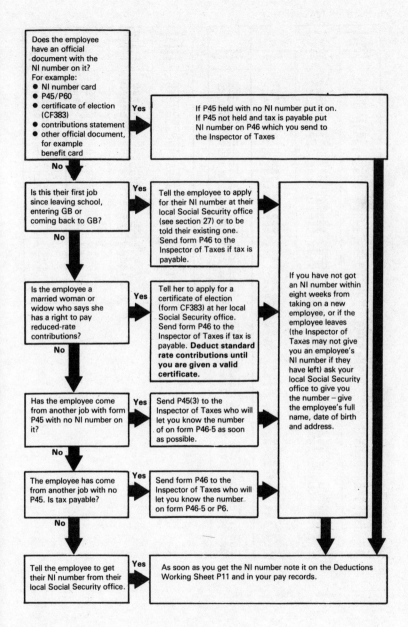

Figure 6.1 *How to get an employee's NI number*

Source: Department of Social Security

Earnings on which employee's contributions payable 1a	Total of employee's and employer's contributions payable 1b	Employee's contributions payable 1c	Employer's contributions*
£	£	£	£
1063	194·05	82·76	111·29
1067	194·83	83·12	111·71
1071	195·61	83·48	112·13
1075	196·39	83·84	112·55
1079	197·16	84·20	112·96
1083	197·94	84·56	113·38
1087	198·72	84·92	113·80
1091	199·50	85·28	114·22
1095	200·28	85·64	114·64
1099	201·05	86·00	115·05
1103	201·83	86·36	115·47
1107	202·61	86·72	115·89
1111	203·39	87·08	116·31
1115	204·17	87·44	116·73
1119	204·94	87·80	117·14
1123	205·72	88·16	117·56
1127	206·50	88·52	117·98
1131	207·28	88·88	118·40
1135	208·06	89·24	118·82
1139	208·83	89·60	119·23
1143	209·61	89·96	119·65
1147	210·39	90·32	120·07
1151	211·17	90·68	120·49
1155	211·95	91·04	120·91
1159	212·72	91·40	121·32
1163	213·50	91·76	121·74
1167	214·28	92·12	122·16
1171	215·06	92·48	122·58
1175	215·84	92·84	123·00
1179	216·61	93·20	123·41
1183	217·39	93·56	123·83
1187	218·17	93·92	124·25
1191	218·95	94·28	124·67
1195	219·73	94·64	125·09
1199	220·50	95·00	125·50
1203	221·28	95·36	125·92
1207	222·06	95·72	126·34
1211	222·84	96·08	126·76
1215	223·62	96·44	127·18
1219	224·39	96·80	127·59
1223	225·17	97·16	128·01
1227	225·95	97·52	128·43
1231	226·73	97·88	128·85
1235	227·51	98·24	129·27
1239	228·28	98·60	129·68
1243	229·06	98·96	130·10
1247	229·84	99·32	130·52
1251	230·62	99·68	130·94
1255	231·40	100·04	131·36
1259	232·17	100·40	131·77
1263	232·95	100·76	132·19
1267	233·73	101·12	132·61
1271	234·51	101·48	133·03
1275	235·29	101·84	133·45
1279	236·06	102·20	133·86
1283	236·84	102·56	134·28
1287	237·62	102·92	134·70
1291	238·40	103·28	135·12
1295	239·18	103·64	135·54
1299	239·95	104·00	135·95

Earnings on which employee's contributions payable 1a	Total of employee's and employer's contributions payable 1b	Employee's contributions payable 1c	Employer's contributions*
£	£	£	£
1303	240·73	104·36	136·37
1307	241·51	104·72	136·79
1311	242·29	105·08	137·21
1315	243·07	105·44	137·63
1319	243·84	105·80	138·04
1323	244·62	106·16	138·46
1327	245·40	106·52	138·88
1331	246·18	106·88	139·30
1335	246·96	107·24	139·72
1339	247·73	107·60	140·13
1343	248·51	107·96	140·55
1347	249·29	108·32	140·97
1351	250·07	108·68	141·39
1355	250·85	109·04	141·81
1359	251·62	109·40	142·22
1363	252·40	109·76	142·64
1367	253·18	110·12	143·06
1371	253·96	110·48	143·48
1375	254·74	110·84	143·90
1379	255·51	111·20	144·31
1383	256·29	111·56	144·73
1387	257·07	111·92	145·15
1391	257·85	112·28	145·57
1395	258·63	112·64	145·99
1399	259·40	113·00	146·40
1403	260·18	113·36	146·82
1407	260·77	113·63	147·14
1409	260·96	113·72	147·24

* for information only — **Do not** enter on P11

Table 6.1 *Monthly table (5 October 1989 to 5 April 1990)*

Source: Department of Social Security, NI not-contracted out contributions, CF 391

employees, and unfortunately they sometimes have a different NI number from the one you hold. If your tax office tells you to use a different NI number, and the employee is over statutory retirement age, or the number is only slightly different from the one you have, use the number the Inland Revenue give you. Where, however, the number is very different from the one you hold, the DSS request that you notify them and ask for confirmation of the correct number.

Percentage rates

Many employers now have quite sophisticated software on their own computer systems to calculate tax, NI, SSP and SMP. Software systems will usually make calculations using percentages rather than tables, and because of this the DSS allows employers to use exact percentages when calculating NI. The tables issued to employers give figures for NI on rounded-up figures, and not for each penny earned. The monthly tables will normally go up in multiples of £4 and it is the next figure below the actual earnings that you look at to see the NI due. For example, as shown in Table 6.1, if earnings for the month were £1146 then contributions would be deducted based on £1143, the next lower figure in the tables. Where exact percentages are used then NI would be calculated exactly on £1146, together with any pennies in the system. Employers who use computer systems will always need to use a calculator to check the NI, as the tables will give a different figure from that calculated by the software, but the difference will be no more than 18p for employees and 21p for employers. It is also unacceptable to mix exact percentages with the table figures for the same employee. Where employers use the exact percentage method and include pennies in the calculation of gross pay, then at the end of the year the gross pay figure can be rounded down to the nearest whole pound.

7
Categories of Employee

Employees under 16

No National Insurance Contributions (NICs) are due from either the employee or the employer for any employee who is aged under 16, but any payments made on or after the sixteenth birthday, including amounts earned before that birthday, are subject to NI.

As an employer you should always make sure that you have the correct date of birth for any new young employee, as contributions must be deducted as soon as the sixteenth birthday is reached. Because of the limited right of recovery of under-deducted NI the employer may not be able to recover from the employee all the NI which is due if he misses this birthday. This will always be the case if no NICs are taken from the birthday up to 5 April; the employer will have to pay for NICS he should have deducted.

Employees over pension age

NICs do not have to be paid by employees on any earnings due to be paid on or after the state pension age (65 for men and 60 for women). If the payments made are earnings, as opposed to true pension, then as the employer you must continue to pay your share of NICs in the normal way. These contributions are obtained using not contracted-out Table C.

It is sometimes difficult to establish whether an employee has actually reached state pension age, as it is not unusual for people to be evasive about their real age. As it is always the employer's responsibility to deduct the correct contribution, if you are in any doubt about an employee's age, you should ask him to apply to the local DSS office for a certificate of age exception, Form CF384. It is always possible to repay overpaid contributions to an employee if this is in the same tax year as they were deducted, so if you are in any doubt about an employee's age, carry on deducting contributions until proof of age is obtained. If an employee for whom you hold a certificate of age exception leaves, you should return the certificate to the employee, or otherwise send it to your local Social Security office.

Students

There is no special NI concession for students employed whether during the vacation or not. Contributions are due from both the employee and the employer.

Married women and widows

There are certain married women and widows who have the right to pay NI at a reduced rate. Until 1977 married women had the right to choose whether or not to continue to pay at the full rate or at a special reduced rate. Payment at the reduced rate limited their entitlement to many state benefits. The right to make this choice no longer exists. Married women now can not elect to pay a reduced rate of NI, and the number of married women who still retain the right to pay the reduced rate is falling.

If a woman tells you that she pays a reduced contribution, then you need to ask for evidence of this. There are a number of certificates still in use, some of which are quite old forms, so they need to be looked at carefully to ensure that they are valid. Old certificates CF380 and CF380A are no longer valid and should not be accepted as the right to pay reduced-rate NI. There are, however, a number of forms (namely CF383) which may still be valid, subject to a few further checks.

A woman may have had a valid certificate returned to her when she left her previous job, but if she has not worked and earned enough to pay NIC for two consecutive tax years, she will have lost the right to pay the reduced rate. In addition, if a woman's marriage has ended by divorce or annulment, then she immediately loses the right to pay reduced rate NI. If after the initial payment a widow does not become entitled to Widow's Benefit, or she loses her right to Widow's Benefit (unless this is because she remarries), then again the right to pay reduced-rate NI is lost.

If a new employee brings you a certificate of election, and you are in any doubt about its validity or the woman's circumstances, you should ask her to exchange it at her local DSS office for a new Form CF383. You should deduct NI at the full rate until such time as she obtains a valid certificate. When a valid certificate is received, adjustments can be made to her NI contributions to refund the over-deduction, provided this is in the same tax year that the deductions were made. For deductions made in a previous year the woman will need to contact her local Department of Social Security (DSS) office for any refund. It is, of course, possible for existing employees to lose the right to pay reduced-rate NI, and employers need to be aware of this possibility. Women whose circumstances change should inform their personnel or payroll office, but very often they are unaware of the way their personal circumstances can affect their NICs. The circumstances in which the right to pay reduced-rate NICs is lost are as follows:

1. if the woman is divorced or her marriage is annulled;
2. if the woman is widowed and after the initial period does not become entitled to Widow's Benefit;
3. if she loses her right to Widow's Benefit (unless this is because she re-marries);
4. if she has no earnings on which NICs have been paid for two consecutive tax years.

Once a woman has lost her right to pay the reduced rate, that right cannot be renewed. It is important for employers to have good communications with employees on this point, as there have been problems where women have become divorced and the employer is not aware of this until there is a re-marriage or a change of name. In some cases where it was shown that the woman had in fact reported her divorce to someone at work, the employer was found to be liable for several years' under-deduction of NI. The DSS now recognise that this can be a problem, and accept that if an organisation has a set procedure for passing this information to payroll, the woman herself, not the employer, may be liable for her increased contributions, if it can be shown she has not followed the correct procedure. It is a good idea, therefore, for employers to check each year with all the women who have reduced-rate certificates that their circumstances have not changed.

A woman can voluntarily give up her right to pay reduced-rate NI. In this event she will normally ask you for a certificate of election which should be returned to the DSS. If there are women within your organisation who are part-time and fall into the lower paid category, it is worthwhile mentioning to them that the full-rate liability on the first band of earnings is now only 2 per cent, thus it may be advantageous for them to elect not to pay the reduced rate (and so obtain only reduced benefits). The difference in NI will need to be worked out and factors such as the woman's age considered. Any woman concerned about this should seek advice from her local DSS office before making any decision.

When a woman for whom you hold a certificate of election leaves, then you should return this to her. This should also be done when a woman reaches the age of 60 or she has not paid NI contributions with you for two consecutive tax years.

Workers from abroad

When an employee arrives from abroad to work for a UK company, then normally NICs are due as from the first pay-day. There is, however, a specific exception to this, where the employees who are not normally resident in the UK and who have been sent to work here for a short period only by overseas employers with places of business outside the UK.

In this case no NICs are payable for the first 52 weeks from the first Sunday following arrival in the UK. If the employee is still here after 52 weeks then normal NI deductions should be made.

Employees from the EC and certain other countries

Normally, employees from the European Community (EC), or foreign countries which have special arrangements with the UK, must pay NI unless they hold a certificate showing that they are still paying the equivalent NICs in their home country.

If you, as an employer, do not have a place of business in the UK, although you may have employees here, you do not voluntarily have to pay employer's NICs. The question of whether a company is seen to have a place of business in the UK can be complicated. If you are in any doubt you should consult your local DSS office, or a professional adviser.

Employees going abroad

If the employer is present or has a place of business in the UK, and has employees who work outside the UK, then for most foreign countries the NI position is explained in leaflet NI132 (*National Insurance for Employers of People Working Abroad*). There are certain countries to which this leaflet does not apply and these are listed in paragraph 127 of the *Employers Manual on National Insurance Contributions, Green Book 1*. There are appropriate leaflets for these countries obtainable from

The DSS Overseas Branch,
Newcastle upon Tyne
NE98 1YX.

This is a complicated subject, and it is often advisable to seek professional advice.

Agency workers

Where employees are employed through an agency, then usually that agency is the employer and liable to deduct NICs. This is not the case if the agency has no place of business or presence in the UK; in that instance the client using the services of the employee is treated as the employer.

There are individuals, hired through agencies, who are treated as employees for NIC purposes. These include actors, singers, entertainers and models. If an employer is in doubt about an employee's status for NI purposes, then he should obtain leaflet NI 192 (*National Insurance for Agencies and People Employed through Agencies*). If you are still in doubt after having read the leaflet you should contact your local DSS office.

Part-time and casual workers

Part-timers and casuals must be considered as employees and you should deduct NI if their income reaches the lower earnings level, even if they are employed by you for only a day or part of a day. The shortest earnings period that can be used is a week, so where the employment is for one, two or three days, up to seven days, it is the weekly NI tables which are used. If you have no NI number for these employees, and are unlikely to get one because of the short duration of the employment, then you can use a temporary NI number made up as follows. The first two letters should be 'TN' (for temporary number) followed by six digits showing the date of birth, for example 210455, followed by M or F for the sex of the individual, so that the NI number would be TN210455F.

Where casual employees are re-employed later in the same week, and this was *not* anticipated on an earlier day, then you may not need to add the two amounts of earnings together for NI purposes. These are treated as separate engagements, and the weekly tables are used to calculate NIC on each separate payment. Where, however, it was envisaged that the employee would work on more than one occasion in the week, and earnings are not paid until the end of that week, then they should be added together to work out NI deductions (see earnings periods in Chapter 6).

People with more than one job

If an employee starts work with you and tells you that he is already paying the maximum NI with another employer, then he need not pay any more contributions with you. You will, however, need to be satisfied that you are not required to deduct NICs, and you should ask the employee to apply to his local DSS office for a deferment of this in respect of the employment with you. The DSS will check whether maximum contributions are payable in the employee's main job and, if so, will issue you with Form RD950 which will authorise you not to deduct any contributions from the employee. Employer's contributions are, however, still payable, and you can obtain these amounts from Table C (either contracted-out or not contracted-out).

An employee who is also self-employed

People who are self-employed normally pay Class 2 contributions, and in addition pay Class 4 contributions which are relative to the amount of their profits. Generally speaking, the Class 2 and Class 4 contributions will be less than the Class 1 contribution that may be payable as an employee. An individual who is self-employed may ask that no Class 1 NIC is deducted from his pay, but employers cannot be authorised to do this. The employee can seek deferment of his self-employed contributions and if after the end of the year he has paid sufficient NIC as an employee, then there may be no further contributions due in respect of his self-employment.

An employee who dies in service

No NIC is due, either employee's or employer's, on the earnings of an employee where the payment of those earnings is made after the date of death.

Directors

The term 'director' refers to a company director in accordance with the 1985 Companies' Act. The normal rules for NI apply to company directors, but there is a separate system based on a yearly earnings period. Full information is given in leaflet NI35 (*National Insurance for Company Directors*). This separate special system must be used for company directors, even where they are paid a regular monthly salary. Where a director is employed throughout the year the contributions deducted will often total approximately the same whether the normal NI procedures are followed or the special directors' NI rules. Difficulties may, however, arise when the director starts with or leaves the company part way through a tax year, or if there is a mid-year change of NIC rates.

Because payments made to directors can sometimes be irregular, it can happen that less than the full amount of NI is payable if the normal tables are used. If, for example, a director was paid the whole of his annual fees in one month, say £30,000, then only one month's NIC would be payable by both him and the employer on that year's earnings. The special system for directors means that where those earnings are the annual earnings, then a full year's NIC will be deducted, even though the payment is made in one month. The calculations can be complicated where an employee becomes a director part way through the year, or changes from not contracted-out to contracted-out NI during the year; in either case reference should be made to leaflet NI35.

8
Payments for NI Purposes

Introduction

Until only a few years ago it was possible to say that wages were subject to National Insurance (NI) as they were to tax. However, a whole range of expenses and benefits were beginning to complicate areas for income tax purposes but did not seem to touch the NI regime. This is no longer the case.

Where a benefit is made available to an employee 'in kind' there can be no NI liability, but where the benefit is provided in cash, or by settling the employee's bill, then NI liability does arise. There is a similar position with payments of expenses to employees, if they are reimbursements of actual expenses incurred, then as with the tax concession, no NI will be due where the expenses are paid out in carrying out the job. It now falls on employers to consider whether there is any 'profit element' in any payment of expenses, and where there is, to identify it and subject it to NI.

The Department of Social Security (DSS) say that this recent view is in no way a reflection of any change in their regulations, but it is certainly a broader interpretation of them. The new manual on NI for employers, NI269, or *Green Book 1*, contains 105 items which the DSS consider are (and in a few exceptions are not) part of gross pay for NI purposes. As already mentioned, when asked at conferences whether there is an easy way to determine whether someone is taxable, my usual reply is 'Is he breathing?' With the new DSS rules, a similar criterion applies to NI, and the easiest option for employers from 6 April 1989 is to say that if an employee gets the benefit in cash, or the expense cannot be seen to be actually spent, then everything is subject to NI – unless it is specifically excluded.

The DSS feel they are being generous to employers by suggesting that if the guidelines in *Green Book 1* are put into operation from 6 April 1989, then no retrospective NICs will be sought for earlier years. Employers are therefore advised to reconsider the NI liability on all their expenses and benefits payments to staff and to make the necessary changes in their payroll procedures.

This change in procedure will often mean a change in payment method by companies, so that payments previously dealt with through the cashier's office, for example, may be better dealt with through the payroll system. In this way, tax and NIC, where appropriate, can be dealt with correctly and at the right time. The DSS assume this to be an easy transition for employers, but even large companies who have been involved in the negotiation of this changeover have spent periods in excess of a year. Local authorities are particularly affected by some of the new rules published by the DSS and, of course, in changing their payment systems, approval of council and often union negotiation is usually required, which can be a lengthy process.

Audit teams from both the Inland Revenue and the DSS are looking at areas where they consider NI could be underpaid. This is a serious warning to employers to correct matters sooner rather than later.

Salaries and wages

Employers should be in no doubt that the full amount of any salary and wages is subject to NI, with the limitation of the maximum contribution for employees. The major difference between taxable and pay subject to NIC is that approved pension contributions deductible before tax is computed are not to be deducted from pay before NI is worked out.

Holiday pay

Where an employer pays holiday pay to his employees, these payments form part of gross pay for NI purposes. If the employer is in the construction industry and has a special scheme for holiday pay, for example where stamps are bought in a holiday pay fund, then there are special rules for these schemes. Depending upon the type of scheme involved, the treatment for NI purposes may vary, and employers should check the rules of the scheme carefully to see what treatment should be applied. There is some guidance in *Green Book 1*, paragraphs 66 and 67.

Holiday pay is one of the areas of NI that is more complicated than it appears. The easiest way to avoid any complications is, as mentioned before, to pay employees monthly salaries, so that where holidays are taken this will not alter what you pay each month. The complications arise where people are paid weekly and would normally want holiday pay in advance, so that they can spend it during their holiday. There are two ways of working out NI contributions when two, three or more weeks' money are paid together. These are called Method A and Method B.

1. *Method A.* The payments of earnings and holiday pay are treated as separate weeks' money paid at the right time. This means that NI contributions are worked out separately for each week's payment and added together so that the total is deducted from the gross payment of earnings and holiday pay paid in advance.
2. *Method B.* The payments of earnings and holiday pay are added together and divided by the number of weeks to which they relate. This figure is then looked up in the weekly tables to find the NI due, which is multiplied by the number of weeks the total was divided by.

The difference between the two methods is that Method A will give a more accurate NI contribution based on individual amounts of earnings and holiday pay for separate weeks, whereas Method B will simply average out the payment to be made. The different results are shown in Table 8.1.

Table 8.1 *Calculations of NI on holiday pay, showing differences resulting from Method A and Method B*

| | | NIC | |
		Total	Employee
Method A	£	£	£
Earnings	175	34.13	15.79
Holiday pay, Week 1	150	27.08	13.54
Holiday pay, Week 2	105	14.76	7.38
		75.97	36.71
Method B			
Earnings	175		
Holiday pay, Week 1	150		
Holiday pay, Week 2	105		
	430		
$\frac{430}{3} = 143.33$		25.82 × 3	12.91 × 3
		77.46	38.73

You will see from Table 8.1 that the method used can alter the contribution payable, and employees would normally wish to pay as little NI as possible. You will be pleased to know that employers are able to choose which method to use, and will normally choose the cheaper. This can be done each time holiday pay is paid, and for each employee. The more sophisticated computerised systems can automatically make this choice for you, if programmed to do so.

Further complications arise where extra payments are made during the holiday period, for example overtime or a bonus. If an extra payment is to be made after the calculations of holiday pay, then you must continue to apply the same method that you used originally. The rule is that if you have used Method A and identified separate weeks, you are able to add in the extra payment in the week in which it is to be paid. Where, however, you have used Method B, you do not unscramble and re-do the calculation, but pay the extra payment as a separate amount. Examples of this are given in the NI manual, *Green Book 1*, paragraph 72.

Bonus, overtime and commission payments

Bonus payments, overtime and commission all count as pay for NI purposes, and should be included with earnings at the time of payment.

Meal allowances and meal vouchers

If meal allowances are paid in cash, or by voucher exchangeable in whole or in part for cash, then these must be included in gross pay for NI purposes. If the vouchers that employees receive can only be exchanged for food or drink, then these need not be included in gross pay, whatever the amount.

Tips and service charges

The deciding factor for NI is whether the employer receives and controls how the money is to be shared out between employees. Where the money from tips passes through the employer's hands, and the employer decides who shall receive how much, then NI is due. Where, however, the tips go straight to the employee, and the employer has no say in how they should be shared out, then no NI is due. The inclusion of a tip on a credit card payment can give rise to problems, as the amount then comes through the employer's till. If this method gives him the control over the distribution of the tips then they are subject to NI. Amounts of service charges that will normally be paid out by the employer are subject to NI as part of gross pay irrespective of who pays or shares out the money.

Give as you earn

Although there is a tax concession for certain amounts of payments to charities handled through payroll, there is no similar concession for NI.

Pension or superannuation contributions

Contributions by employees into an approved pension or superannuation scheme are, subject to certain limits, deducted from gross pay for tax purposes. There is no similar concession for NI purposes, and the full amount of gross pay is subject to NI deductions.

Payments in kind

A true payment in kind is not subject to NI. The DSS now make a distinction between payments in kind that can be turned into cash by surrender, and those that can be turned into cash by sale. Those that can be surrendered for cash, eg premium bonds, national savings certificates or certain securities, are to be included in gross pay for NI purposes.

By using a payment in kind an employer can quite legitimately bypass the NI system. A payment in kind must, however, be exactly that, so that the *goods* are given to the employee and not the *cash* to buy those goods. This means that an employer must give directly to the employee the television set or the golf club subscription, and not simply pay the employee's bill for those items. The employer can give the employee a voucher to obtain goods and services, and this will not be subject to NI, provided the voucher can only be exchanged for goods and services and not for cash, or partly for goods and cash.

Reimbursed expenses

Provided that expenses are actually incurred by the employee in the course of carrying out his job, any amount of reimbursed expense can be excluded from gross pay for NI. The reimbursement of actual expenses will solve both the tax and NI problems and as a bonus the employer will have the relevant bills and receipts on which he will be able to reclaim VAT.

Round sum expenses

In a similar way as for tax, round sum expenses must be included in gross pay for NI purposes. If the employee can demonstrate that he has actually spent some of the round sum on an actual business expense, then that part can be excluded for NI, and the balance unaccounted for duly subjected to NI. The DSS use the term 'specific and distinct' payments of expenses actually incurred, and this clearly would exclude any 'round sum' payment.

Travelling and subsistence allowances

It has already been said that an actual reimbursement of expenses incurred attracts no NI, and a round sum not supported by bills or receipts is subject to NI. If an employer wants to have a system that falls somewhere between these two extremes, then he must fulfil certain conditions laid down by the DSS. These are that

1. the scheme you develop has no overall element of profit;
2. the payments are based on an accurate survey of the costs involved;
3. the scheme is designed to accommodate movements in prices;
4. the payments made are reasonable in relation to the employment(s) involved;
5. a claim is made by your employee covering each item of expense.

Employers should note that even though they may have an Inland Revenue dispensation for expenses (see Chapter 4), this will not apply for NI, unless the above five conditions are also fulfilled. Employers will probably have simplified their system, following an Inland Revenue dispensation, and will not therefore have the type of controls that the DSS require. This means that payments of expenses which are free from tax could be subject to NI.

This is particularly true for 'working rule agreements' where the Inland Revenue may have accepted that there is no profit element in the expense paid. These payments will be subject to NI unless there is a properly controlled system of monitoring the payments to show that there is no profit element for NI.

Telephone expenses

Where the employer contracts with British Telecom to put a telephone in an employee's home, then this is a true payment in kind for the employee and attracts no NI liability. In the usual case where the employee contracts directly with British Telecom, or another provider, for a telephone, and the employer reimburses him for the cost, the payment is liable for contributions. The DSS rules are quite clear that where any part of the rental of a private telephone is reimbursed by an employer, this is subject to NI. Only individually-logged business calls can be paid by the employer without being subject to NI contributions.

Season tickets

Where an employer provides a season ticket for an employee, NI liability can be quite easily avoided. The season ticket must become a 'payment in kind' (see page 79), so that it is purchased directly by the employer and given to the employee. NI will be due where the employer gives the money to the employee to buy the season ticket or reimburses the employee for that expense.

Relocation expenses

In this area also the DSS use the words 'specific and distinct', so that any round sum or general expense allowance paid to employees for relocation expenses are subject to NI. Where, however, the employee provides bills, eg for solicitor's and estate agent's fees, these can be paid without NI deductions. Where the employer has set up a relocation policy for expenses, then similar rules must apply as for expenses schemes generally as noted above for season tickets, telephone, etc.

Statutory Sick Pay and Statutory Maternity Pay

Both SSP and SMP are subject to NI in the normal way.

9
Starters and Leavers for NI Purposes

Introduction

The Department of Social Security (DSS) have similar rules to the Inland Revenue for deciding who, for National Insurance (NI) purposes, is an employee. Employers will encounter problems with both these departments if they treat people as being self-employed consultants when they are their employees (see Chapter 3). For NI purposes, an employee is someone who will be charged to Schedule E income tax, who is also under a 'contract of service' or who is an office-holder. In addition, several categories of people are treated as employees, including office cleaners, agency workers, certain lecturers, a husband employed by his wife, or a wife employed by her husband.

Starters

NI numbers
An employer needs a NI number for each employee; details of how to find the number or how to make a temporary NI number are given in Chapter 6.

When an employee is taken on, the decision will have been made regarding the intervals at which he will be paid. This interval is set, even though the employee may work for only a few days before his first pay-day. Where, for example, an employee is to be paid monthly and starts work on, say, 24 April, the earnings from 24 April to 30 April, although this represents one week's pay, are included in a monthly earnings period for the calculation of NI. Similarly, with a weekly paid employee, pay for two or three days' work is included in a weekly earnings period calculation.

It is the employer's duty to deduct the correct rate of NI, and because of this employers are advised, for new employees, to take standard category A contributions in all cases where there is any doubt as to the correct category to be used. If the employee later provides a certificate of deferment or certificate of election, then the contributions overpaid can be recalculated and any refund made, provided this is in the same tax year. Contributions that may have been overpaid in a closed tax year can be reclaimed by the employee and employer from the DSS.

Leavers

Employees may leave employment halfway through the week or month for which they would normally be paid. As has already been stressed, the first and most important consideration is that the payroll department are informed when an employee leaves, so they can ensure that regular salary and other payments are stopped at the appropriate time.

A similar situation arises with the calculation of NI for leavers as for starters, and the normal earnings period is used. This means that if a monthly paid employee leaves employment on the seventh day of the month, his NIC is calculated using the monthly tables, even though he will have only received one week's money.

Pay in lieu of notice
Where the amount being paid is a true payment in lieu of notice there is no NI liability. Payment in lieu of notice would normally be the wages for the notice period laid down in the contract of employment.

Golden handshakes, etc
Where a payment could be described as an inducement payment, in other words to recruit or retain staff, then the DSS see these as arising from the employment and are therefore subject to NI. Employers are instructed to contact the DSS if they think that such a payment should not be included in gross pay.

Redundancy pay
Where the payments are of genuine redundancy pay under a properly constructed scheme, then normally no NI will be due. Where the payments amount to a golden handshake, then the DSS may consider that NI is due, as the payment is an inducement in respect of the employment.

Part Three:
Statutory Sick Pay and Statutory Maternity Pay

10
Statutory Sick Pay

Introduction

Statutory Sick Pay (SSP) has been around long enough for most employers to consider that they know all the basic rules. Unfortunately this is not always the case as the rules are complicated and the Department of Social Security (DSS) assume that all employers have an unlimited amount of time to study their manuals. With all statutory requirements of employers, you should ensure that the most recent government-issued booklets are used. The current issue of the employer's manual on SSP is leaflet NI270 (or *Green Book 2*), from April 1989. In addition you will need the tables of dates and rates of payment for the current year, leaflet SSP55 or *Red Book 2*. To make life more colourful for employers the DSS have introduced *Yellow Book K* or leaflet NI268 from April 1989 which is an employer's key and quick guide to National Insurance Contributions (NIC) and SSP, being some 20 pages long. If all else fails, employers can dial the DSS Freephone advice line on 0800 393 539.

Statutory Sick Pay does not in any way affect any requirements which an employer may have under his occupational sick-pay scheme. The two schemes normally run together, so that if employees are entitled to full pay under the occupational sick-pay scheme, this is not enhanced by any SSP, but employers can treat part of the payment they make as being in respect of SSP provided it is paid for the same period, and reclaim this part from the government. From the employee's point of view, if he is within a full occupational sick-pay scheme, he will only be interested in the fact that his normal pay continues while he is sick, and may not be aware that part of this is deemed to be SSP which his employer is paying on behalf of the government.

For employees not covered by any occupational sick-pay scheme, then the SSP scheme means that instead of receiving no pay at all for days when they are sick, there may be entitlement to a payment of SSP made by the employer.

Before SSP was introduced, employees usually had to submit medical certificates from their doctor to their local DSS office, where an amount of sickness benefit was calculated and paid to the employee, normally by Giro. The SSP scheme simply passed this burden of calculation and payment from the government to employers, and involved employers in yet another complex scheme of rules.

Employees covered by the SSP scheme

For SSP purposes, someone is an employee if his earnings attract a liability for Class 1 NIC, or would do if the earnings were high enough. The employer, for the purposes of SSP, is whoever is liable to pay the employer's share of Class I contributions. Thus new employers very soon find out that there is far more to the job than merely paying wages at the end of the week or month.

There are certain categories of employee which require a particular mention and these are as follows:

1. *Directors.* Directors are employees of the company and are therefore within the SSP scheme.
2. *Agency workers.* This is a difficult area, but generally people who work for employment agencies will not be covered by the SSP scheme, because the contract of employment will normally terminate at the end of each week or when there is no work available. Where the employment with the agency becomes more continuous, and there are likely to be weekly fixed-term contracts, then there may be some liability for SSP. Where the contracts are with the same employer and separated by not more than eight weeks, then the two contracts either side of the break can be added together to see if they exceed 13 weeks. If they do then SSP will need to be paid but only in the short term as the contract will be due to end probably at the end of the week.

   Employees who work for agencies and cannot receive SSP may be entitled to Sickness Benefit which is payable by the DSS. If you, as the employer, are an employment agency then not only will you need to examine the rules very carefully, but if you cannot pay SSP, issue Form SP1 and advise your employees to fill in Form SC1 and send it to their local DSS office. They may be able to claim Sickness Benefit instead.
3. *Foreign-going mariners.* If a UK employer pays a special rate of NI contribution for foreign-going mariners then the SSP scheme does not cover these employees.

4. *Home-trade mariners.* These employees, if employed by a UK employer, may be covered by the SSP scheme, but there are special rules for days of sickness outside the EC. SSP will not be paid if the employee is first sick while outside the EC.
5. *Aircrew and continental shelf-workers.* In general terms these people are covered by the SSP scheme.

Evidence of sickness or incapacity for work

The heading for this section identifies two reasons why employees may be incapable of working for you, and sickness and incapacity for work are not necessarily the same thing. For the purposes of SSP, compassionate leave, where the employee himself is not incapable of work, does not entitle the employee to payment of SSP.

In the first instance an employer has to decide what evidence he needs from his employees in support of their notification that they are sick. Your employees need to know what steps they have to take in notifying you; most employers have a sick notification procedure laid down in the conditions of work. Employees are often required to telephone their employers on the first day that they are unable to work, and if they are away from work because of sickness for one to seven days, most employers allow a system of 'self-certification'. Over seven days, employers would normally require a medical certificate or similar statement signed by the employee's doctor.

As an employer you need to decide what evidence of sickness you will accept, as this may be presented to you in a variety of ways. Medical certificates can come from various people other than medical practitioners, for example from an osteopath or acupuncturist, and you will need to take a reasoned view when these are presented to you. Incapacity for work for SSP purposes means that the employee is unable to carry out the job in respect of which he has a contract of employment. It is therefore possible for an employee whose job is to do close detailed work, who normally wears glasses or contact lenses, to be incapacitated for work because these have been lost or broken. It is the employer's decision in these circumstances, having regard to all the facts available, to accept whether a person is unable to work.

Incapacity for work is normally considered to be a whole day, so if somebody goes sick after having arrived for work, that day can only be treated as a day of incapacity provided no work has been done. There are other reasons for deemed incapacity and these are, for example, where a doctor considers that somebody convalescing is unable to work, or where the person has been certified as the carrier of an infectious disease and has been advised not to go to work. You may also treat it as incapacity if a pregnant woman does not attend work because there are cases of German measles among the people with whom she normally works.

As it is up to the employer to decide whether the evidence or reason given by the employee is acceptable, there are occasions when the employer may decide not to pay SSP. Larger firms may well have welfare or personnel officers with whom the employee can discuss things, but in smaller firms an employee will usually ask the manager directly for his reasons for not paying SSP. If matters cannot be resolved following these discussions, your employee has the right to ask you for a written statement, and may then ask for the matter to be decided by the adjudicating officer at the local DSS office. The adjudicating officer will look at documentary evidence, which will include the employer's written statement. Because of this procedure, employers should have more than a general feeling of suspicion about the period of sickness which led to the decision not to pay SSP: in other words, they should be certain that they have a good case to present to the DSS.

Qualifying days

Once you have decided to accept your employee's evidence that he is unable to work, you then have to consider whether any SSP will be payable.

Qualifying days are the only days for which SSP can be paid, but not all of these days will necessarily be payment days. An employer can choose which days of the week are to be qualifying days, provided that both the employer and the employees agree. Most employers would have made this choice when SSP was first introduced. The usual working days in the week will count as qualifying days, for example Monday to Friday inclusive, or where business is open on Saturday, the qualifying days would be Monday to Saturday. An employer may choose to have every day of the week as a qualifying day and as SSP weeks start on Sunday, this would be Sunday to Saturday inclusive. Many large employers have a seven-day qualifying week, as this can make some calculations easier, and such a system will accommodate a variety of employees with different working weeks.

If employees regularly work alternate weeks, then you must have at least one qualifying day in each week, so you need to agree with those employees which day or days in the week in which they are not required to work are qualifying days. Where working patterns are irregular and you are unable to agree on qualifying days, if you can both agree that Sunday is a rest day, then the qualifying days will be Monday to Saturday inclusive.

Period of Incapacity for Work (PIW)

Having established that an employee is sick, and that he has been sick on qualifying days, you need to establish if there is a Period of Incapacity for Work (PIW). A PIW only occurs where an employee is incapable of work for at least four consecutive days. These can be any days of the week. If the employee is sick over the weekend period which would not normally be classed as two working days, you will need to ask whether the employee was sick for the four days, and not just for the Friday and the following Monday. If there are less than four days of sickness together, then there is no PIW. For any SSP to be paid there must be a PIW; absences of sickness which do not make a PIW can never have SSP paid for them. For periods less than four days, many employers will have occupational sick-pay schemes, so that employees continue to receive normal pay for short periods of sickness. Personnel departments in large firms usually keep a check on all these odd days, together with longer periods of sickness, and as a welfare matter would probably ask to see an employee who is continually absent from work owing to sickness.

Linked PIWs

Once an employer has established that a PIW exists, the next question to be looked at is whether the employee has a previous PIW within the last eight weeks or, in the case of a new employee, whether he has a previous PIW within the last eight weeks at his former job. If he has been working for you in excess of eight weeks, your payroll records should indicate when any previous PIW ended. In order for PIWs to link together there must be a period between the two PIWs of eight weeks (56 days) or less. Once again, the DSS help employers with this counting with a booklet of dates which is issued each year, leaflet SSP55 or *Red Book 2*. This booklet quite simply sets out for the first day of each PIW the earliest linking date of any previous PIW. It is only PIWs that are linked in this way. Periods of sickness of one, two or three days can never be used for the purposes of linking PIWs together.

When a new employee falls sick within the first eight weeks then you will need to ask him if he has a leaver's statement from his previous employer. This is Form SSP1(L) and will have been given to him when he had last reported sick in his previous employment. (You may have to prepare this form when an employee leaves you, and this is explained later in this chapter.) It will come as no surprise to employers that Form SSP1(L) is one of the least-used forms in the SSP system, simply because most employees when they take a job with a new employer are not likely to admit to any sickness with their last employer. Because of this forms SSP1(L) are rarely handed to the new employer.

Employees for whom no SSP can be paid

Some employees may not be entitled to SSP but may be able to claim a Social Security Benefit instead. Once an employer has decided for one of the following reasons that SSP cannot be paid at the start of a PIW, then the employee cannot receive SSP for any part of that PIW. If SSP cannot be paid at the start of the first PIW, should the PIWs link together then SSP cannot be paid for any of the linking PIWs.

An employee cannot get SSP if on the first day of a PIW:

1. The PIW links with a claim to a Social Security Benefit, namely Sickness Benefit, Invalidity Benefit, Severe Disablement Allowance or Maternity Allowance (MA). You will normally know from your records whether any of these benefits may have been paid and employers should ask the employee for a linking letter given to them by the DSS. You will also know if you have issued Form SSP1 to an employee if you have a linked PIW that you were unable to pay SSP for. If an employee does not give you the SSP1, or the linking letter from the DSS, or you are in any doubt about a previous payment of Social Security Benefit, then you are advised to contact your local Social Security office and explain the problem to them. Employers should always be careful of paying SSP when this may not be due, as overpayments will not be recoverable from the DSS.

2. The employee has already had 28 weeks SSP from you or his previous employer and the leaver's statement that he brings to you (Form SSP1(L)) details this, and the PIW with you links with the last day of the PIW with the previous employer. (You will know whether you have already paid 28 weeks SSP as you will have issued Form SSP1 to the employee when that occurred, having checked whether the last PIW with you linked with this new PIW.)

3. The average weekly earnings are below the lower earnings level for NI. Average earnings are calculated by adding together the gross pay for NI purposes in the eight weeks ending with the last pay-day before the start of the PIW and dividing this by 8 to give an average weekly wage. For monthly paid employees you will need to add together the payments made on the last normal pay-day before the PIW started, and any other payments made in the eight weeks ending with that payment (usually two months' salary), multiply that figure by 6 and divide by 52 to obtain an average weekly wage. These calculations of average earnings are the same as for SMP purposes.

   Once the average earnings calculation has been done for a PIW, it is not recalculated, even though the employee's earnings may change during that PIW. If PIWs are linked together then the average earnings calculations done at the start of the first PIW count for all the linked PIWs.

4. The employee is under a contract of service for a specified period of three months or less. If, however, at the end of the three months the employee is kept on, so that the contract exceeds the original three months, then SSP will become payable but only for periods after the end of the initial three months. Where short contracts occur with the same employer, and these are separated by not more than eight weeks, then these contracts are counted together for SSP purposes, depending on when the PIW starts. These special rules are complicated: if after reading *Green Book 2*, paragraph 61, you are in any doubt, contact your local Social Security office.

5. The employees are over retirement age (60 for women and 65 for men). If the employee is over retirement age on the first day of the PIW then no SSP can be paid. PIWs that link together are counted as one PIW, so if a PIW starts after retirement age, and links with an earlier PIW that started before retirement age, then SSP can continue to be paid for as long as that PIW lasts, or for as long as any new PIW links back with one that started before retirement age. If you are in any doubt as to your employee's age then you should always check this with your local DSS office.

6. The employee is pregnant and entitled to Statutory Maternity Pay (SMP). An employer cannot pay SSP to an employee for a period of 18 weeks before and after her baby is due to be born. This 18-week period starts with either:

   - the beginning of the week she is first entitled to SMP from you, or
   - the beginning of the week she is first entitled to MA from the DSS (you may need to ask your local DSS whether the woman has claimed MA, or
   - the beginning of the sixth week before the Expected Week of Confinement (EWC), if she is not entitled to either SMP or MA.

   Even though the woman may decide to remain at work after the sixth week before the EWC, her right to SSP for 18 weeks starts from the beginning of the sixth week before the EWC. This means that although SMP may be paid for less than the maximum 18 weeks, there is still a full 18 weeks in which no SSP can be paid.

7. The employee is absent from work because of a trade dispute. If an employee on the first day of a PIW is involved in a strike or lock-

out, or any other dispute about work, then no SSP can be paid for that PIW. This will not be the case if the particular employee did not take any part in the strike up to and including the first day of the PIW, always remembering that PIWs link, and it is the first day of the initial PIW that is looked at for this purpose.

8. The employee is in legal custody. If on the first day of PIW an employee is being kept in custody by the police or in prison, then no SSP is payable. (Note that helping the police with their enquiries is not the same as being in legal custody.)

9. The employee is outside the European Community (EC). On the first day of a PIW if the employee is outside the EC then no SSP is payable for any of the PIW.

10. If the employee falls sick on the first day of work with you. In this case, no work has been done under the contract of employment, and no SSP can be paid. This will apply if the employee reports sick instead of turning up for work on his first day. If, however, he turns up and does even a few minutes work on that first day, SSP is payable.

In all these circumstances the employer cannot pay SSP, although there may be a PIW. Form SSP1 is to be issued to the employee no later than seven days after the notification of sickness. Form SSP1 contains a series of headings so that the employer can tick the appropriate reason, as in 1–10 above, who no SSP can be paid.

Waiting days

The first three qualifying days of a PIW are waiting days and no payment can be made until after these three days. If PIWs link together then the first three qualifying days of the first PIW are waiting days, and the second or subsequent PIW will not contain any further waiting days. If a second PIW does not link with an earlier PIW, then three waiting days would be counted on each occasion.

For example, if an employee whose qualifying days are Monday to Friday falls sick on a Friday and returns to work on the following Thursday, then the qualifying and waiting days can be identified as in Figure 10.1.

The calculation of SSP involves a series of decisions. For example, you have an employee you have accepted as being sick. He has not been excluded for any of the reasons in the previous section, he has been sick for a PIW, and you know there is no linkage with an earlier PIW. Last, you know what are Qualifying Days (QD). There is now little left to decide

Fri	Sat	Sun	Mon	Tues	Wed	Thur	Fri	Sat	Sun
Q			Q	Q	Q	Q	Q		
W			W	W	✓				

Sick —————————————————⟶

Figure 10.1 *Unlinked PIW*

Note: Friday, Monday and Tuesday are 'waiting days' (W), so SSP is payable on Wednesday only. Qualifying days shown with Q.

before payment is actually calculated. SSP is not, however, paid for 'waiting days'.

The DSS supply a working sheet, Form SSP2, which can be very helpful to a new employer who has not calculated SSP in the past. It does help to be able to see which days are qualifying or waiting days, so that the days of payment can be readily identified. In the example given, qualifying days are Monday to Friday, with Saturday and Sunday non-qualifying days, the employee was sick from Friday to the following Wednesday, a period of six days, so that there is a PIW. Waiting days are the first three qualifying days, in this case Friday, Monday and Tuesday, so the only day when payment of SSP is due is Wednesday. If the employee falls sick within the next eight weeks, so that the two PIWs link together, and he falls sick on a Tuesday and returns on the following Monday then this would be as shown in Figure 10.2.

Sat	Sun	Mon	Tues	Wed	Thur	Fri	Sat	Sun	Mon
		Q	Q	Q	Q	Q			Q
			✓	✓	✓	✓			

Sick —————————————————————————⟶

Figure 10.2 *Linked PIW*

Note: There are no 'waiting days (W)' so SSP can be paid for Tuesday to Friday inclusive. Qualifying days shown with Q.

You will see that SSP will be paid for the four days: Tuesday, Wednesday, Thursday, Friday, which are qualifying days without any waiting days as the two PIWs link. You will need to know for your own records whether the employee was actually sick for the Saturday and Sunday and this should be declared on any self-certification form. In this instance it would not make any difference to the payment of SSP if the employee were not sick on the Saturday and Sunday. If, as an employer, you had decided that Saturday and Sunday were also qualifying days then this employee, if he were sick at the weekend, would be paid for six days, ie from Tuesday to Sunday inclusive.

Payment of SSP

Having identified the PIW, all that remains to be done is to work out how much SSP can actually be paid.

Statutory Sick Pay is notified to employers each year as a weekly rate. There are two weekly rates: the standard rate and the lower rate. Employers can find the current weekly rates in *Red Book 2* and a fresh

Table 10.1 *SSP Daily rate tables – standard rate*

£ Unrounded daily rates[a]	No of QDs in week	Standard rate £52.10 (average earnings £84.00 or over per week)						
		1	2	3	4	5	6	7
		£	£	£	£	£	£	£
7.4428	7	7.45	14.89	22.33	29.78	37.22	44.66	52.10
8.6833	6	8.69	17.37	26.05	34.74	43.42	52.10	
10.42	5	10.42	20.84	31.26	41.68	52.10		
13.025	4	13.03	26.05	39.08	52.10			
17.3666	3	17.37	34.74	52.10				
26.05	2	26.05	52.10					
52.10	1	52.10						

[a]Unrounded rates are included for employers with computerised payroll systems.

Source: Department of Social Security, *Red Book 2*

booklet with the revised rates is issued each year in March as the new rates start on 6 April.

Employers need to decide whether the standard rate or lower rate is payable, and this is linked to the average earnings that you will have calculated in deciding whether any SSP at all should be paid. If the average earnings are between the current lower earning level (£43 and £83.99), then the lower rate of SSP is payable. If the average earnings calculation gives a rate of £84 (current level) or over per week then the standard rate of SSP is payable. All these details of average earnings and rates are given in leaflet SSP55, *Red Book 2* each year. Experienced payroll people will know at a glance which rate of SSP is payable and what that rate is.

Having decided whether the standard or the lower rate of SSP is payable, employers need to decide how much is payable per day. SSP is a daily rate, unlike SMP which is only paid for whole weeks. The weekly rate of SSP is divided by the number of qualifying days in the employer's

Table 10.2 *SSP Daily rate tables – lower rate*

£ Unrounded daily rates[a]	No of QDs in week	Standard rate £36.25 (average earnings £43.00–£83.99)						
		1	2	3	4	5	6	7
		£	£	£	£	£	£	£
5.1785	7	5.18	10.36	15.54	20.72	25.90	31.08	36.25
6.0416	6	6.05	12.09	18.13	24.17	30.21	36.25	
7.25	5	7.25	14.50	21.75	29.00	36.25		
9.0625	4	9.07	18.13	27.19	36.25			
12.0833	3	12.09	24.17	36.25				
18.125	2	18.13	36.25					
36.25	1	36.25						

[a]Unrounded rates are included for employers with computerised payroll systems.

Source: Department of Social Security, *Red Book 2*

week. This means that if the qualifying days are Monday to Friday inclusive, then the standard or lower rate of SSP is divided by 5 to give a daily rate. These calculations are done for you in *Red Book 2* so that the daily rate for qualifying days of one to seven in a week are worked out for you. This means you can easily see that if you have, say, three qualifying days in the week and the employee is sick for two days, precisely how much SSP is payable. These daily rate tables are reproduced here as Tables 10.1 and 10.2, so that you can see that this is quite a simple exercise.

Deductions from SSP

Any payment of SSP is treated like pay for tax and NIC purposes, so you would need to add together any normal pay and any SSP payable before the statutory calculations are made.

When to pay SSP

Employers should pay SSP at the same time as they would normally have paid wages or salary for those days. This means that weekly paid people would usually expect to be paid any wages and any days of SSP in their normal wages cheque. Many employees are paid weekly wages one week in arrears, so that SSP can also be paid one week in arrears with any normal pay. As in all matters relating to payroll (as already mentioned), good communication is vital to the system, and the larger an organisation is, the more difficult it is to get information into the payroll department as soon as it is needed. Absences due to sickness are normally dealt with by a personnel department in a large company, so it is very necessary that personnel have good lines of communication with payroll so that SSP can be calculated correctly as quickly as possible.

If an employee has been paid before it is realised that he was sick, then recalculations will need to be done and adjustments made on the next pay-day. For employers with occupational sick-pay schemes, this will normally mean that the employee has had the right amount of money, but that SSP will need to be calculated and recovered from the DSS, and details of the adjustments kept.

If an employer has been in dispute with the employee regarding the payment of SSP, and the DSS adjudication officer has given the employer a formal decision that SSP is to be paid then there will be a time limit for payment.

Mistakes in SSP calculations or payments and how to reclaim SSP and NIC

With any complicated system, mistakes are bound to be made from time to time. If an error is discovered in the same tax year in which it was made, then the error can be put right and any adjustments made. In line with any error made in a payroll office, it is always advisable to leave intact the original figures and simply draw a line through them, writing in any corrections above. Once a payment has been made to an employee, then it is always necessary to be able to see how that payment was calculated, and you will not be able to do this if figures are rubbed out or painted over. If you have paid too much SSP then you can recover this from your employee at the next pay day, and adjust the amount you reclaimed from the DSS in the next month's payslip.

If a mistake is discovered after the end of the tax year on 5 April, it is possible for the employer to adjust his end-of-year returns provided these are still held by the Inland Revenue Accounts Office. However, if the records have all been processed you will need to contact your local DSS office, giving details of the error and asking for advice.

Matters can get more complicated if you find that you have paid SSP when you should not have done, and you will need to notify the DSS of this. This will probably result in a considerable volume of correspondence with the DSS. In addition you will have to consider whether or not you have the right of recovery from your employee. These complications are an incentive to employers to get it right first time, but with such a complicated system this is not always possible.

Employers are paying SSP not out of their own pockets, but on behalf of the government. Therefore, at the end of each month employers can total up the amounts of SSP paid to all their employees and reclaim the whole amount from the government. This is done by deducting the amount of SSP paid for all employees from the NIC due to be paid with each end-of-the-month return (see Chapter 14); the same method is used for SMP (see Chapter 11).

Thus, in theory, SSP should cost the employer nothing, but this, of course, is not always the case. Where the lower rate of SSP is paid, then this will not attract any NIC, but the standard rate of SSP will attract NIC, not only for the employee but also for the employer. In addition, there is the cost of payroll time in the calculation and payment of SSP on behalf of the DSS. As a 'compensation' for this employers are entitled to claim an amount of 'NIC compensation', currently 7.5 per cent of the amount of SSP paid each month. This calculation is done with the returns at the end of each month (see Chapter 14).

What to do when SSP stops

Payment of SSP should stop when:

1. The employee's incapacity for work ends because he either returns to work or there are no further doctor's statements.
2. The contract of service comes to an end (employers are not allowed to terminate a contract of employment simply to avoid the payment of SSP).
3. SSP has been paid for 28 times the weekly rate of SSP. This may be while the employee has been in your employment or while he has been with you and earlier employment(s). In these circumstances a Social Security Benefit may be due.
4. The woman is pregnant and the 18-week disqualifying period starts.
5. PIWs have been linking continuously for three years. These linked PIWs must be in your employment for this condition to be enforced.
6. The employee is taken into legal custody (not simply 'helping the police with their enquiries').
7. The employee leaves the European Community.

Where the employee continues to be sick but you can no longer pay him any SSP because of one of the conditions above, then you need to notify the employee of this on Form SSP1. Form SSP1 will show the last date on which you were able to pay SSP, the date that the sickness started and why you can no longer pay SSP. You will also need to show how many weeks and days of SSP you have paid.

Record-keeping

You are required by law to keep certain records regarding SSP. These are:

1. Dates of sickness lasting at least four calendar days in a row (PIWs).
2. Records of any days within a PIW for which SSP was not paid and why.
3. The qualifying days in each PIW.
4. Any leaver's statements (SSP1(L)) you took into account.
5. A copy of any SSP1(L) issued by you.

The easiest way to keep these records is on Form SSP2, to which you can attach any Form SSP1(L). If you have another method of record-keeping, for example on a computer, then you must keep all the information that is shown on Form SSP2 which you can obtain from your local Social Security office.

In addition to records of sickness you are also required by law to keep records of any payments of SSP. Each employee's deductions working sheet (Form P11) should show the amount of any SSP paid in each pay period, together with all the other pay, tax and NIC details. At the end of each month and at the end of the year, totals of SSP paid are required, as detailed in Chapters 14 and 15.

Control of absences due to sickness

Employers should have some sort of control system so that frequent periods of absence by employees due to sickness can be monitored. This would normally be done by a personnel department in the case of large employers. It sometimes happens that employers can be aware of a problem with sick leave and not know what to do about it. In such cases help is available from the DSS. You would normally apply for help when an employee has had at least four self-certified absences in a period of 12 months, where he has been sick for between four and seven days only. You will need to tell your local Social Security office, the employee's name and address, the name and address of the employee's GP and the dates when he has been sick in the past year or two. You will also need to send the DSS the four self-certificates which should show the nature of the incapacity each time.

The employee's GP may in these circumstances be asked to provide a confidential report to the Regional Medical Service. Employers may, if they wish, suspend payment of SSP on the fifth occasion within 12 months that the employee is sick, and the Regional Medical Service could be asked to give an independent opinion.

There are other problems, apart from frequent periods of sickness, where periods of sickness are lengthier than expected. The *Employer's Manual on SSP* does give information about the number of months certain illnesses or disorders could be expected to last, and employers can seek help from the DSS if periods of illness last longer than those indicated.

Offences and penalties

Because SSP is a statutory requirement of employers, there are penalties for failure by an employer to carry out certain procedures in relation to it. Generally, an offence will give rise to a fine not exceeding £400, and continuing failure to provide information, will result in a fine of £20 for each day that the failure continues. Normally, it would only be the worst cases of failure by employers that would attract such penalties but, of course, it does indicate to employers that all the procedures for SSP must be taken seriously. Employers are certainly advised to contact their local DSS office in any cases of doubt regarding the payment of SSP, and to do this sooner rather than later.

11

Statutory Maternity Pay

Introduction

Statutory Maternity Pay (SMP) is the most recent social security responsibility passed on to employers by the Government. SMP was introduced on 6 April 1987 for babies due to be born on or after 21 June of that year. The scheme is an amalgamation of the Maternity Allowance (MA) system operated by the Department of Social Security (DSS) and the maternity pay scheme run by the Department of Employment. When SMP was introduced, employers had been dealing with Statutory Sick Pay (SSP) quite successfully, so this was an opportunity for the Government to impose a further burden on employers and have them administer another scheme of benefits on their behalf.

One of the problems with MA was that entitlement was based on National Insurance Contributions (NICs) paid in the relevant tax year which could be a year or two before the woman had the baby. The amalgamation of the two schemes achieved the government's intention of allowing women in paid work to give up work for a short time in order to have a baby and receive some government support for the weeks when they were not earning.

Statutory Maternity Pay is paid for a maximum of 18 weeks by an employer and he is able to do this on the same pay-days he would have paid the woman's salary or wages. The rules are quite complicated for employers, and depend upon a woman's length of service with that employer, her earnings and a number of other factors to be dealt with in more detail.

Women who are excluded from the scheme

The first decision an employer has to make is whether the woman qualifies for any benefit at all under the SMP scheme. If she does not, then the employer must issue her with a formal notification of exclusion, giving the reasons for not paying her. The following categories are automatically excluded:

1. Young women below the age of 16.
2. Women aged 60 or over.
3. Women for whom the employer is not liable to pay the employer's share of NIC.
4. Members of Her Majesty's Forces.
5. Foreign-going mariners (stewardesses, etc).
6. Women who are self-employed.

In all these circumstances if the woman claims SMP from you, you should give her Form SMP1, and if she has given you the evidence of her pregnancy as shown in Form MatB1 (which is given to her by her midwife or GP), you should return it to her and tell her she may be able to claim some MA from the DSS. This Form SMP1 is used in several other circumstances where payment cannot be made by you.

Qualifying conditions

Once an employer has decided that a woman is not automatically excluded from the payment of SMP there are still five further conditions which need to be fulfilled before payment can be made.

Employers need to obtain a copy of the *Employer's Guide to Statutory Maternity Pay*, NI257, from the DSS. In the centre of this booklet there is a flow chart which can be used as a quick guide to the basic rules for SMP.

The conditions for entitlement are as follows:

1. The woman must give you notice that she intends to be absent from work because of pregnancy.
2. She must have been employed continuously for at least 26 weeks with you up to and including the Qualifying Week (QW).
3. She must have received average weekly earnings in the eight weeks ending with the last pay-day in or immediately before the QW, equal to at least the NI lower earnings level.
4. She must produce evidence of her expected week of confinement and the employer needs to be satisfied that she has reached the twenty-eighth week of pregnancy or has already had the baby.
5. She must have stopped work for payment of SMP to start.

These five conditions are critical to the payment of SMP and so fuller information is given below. It is also necessary to define what is meant by the QW, and this is the fifteenth week before the Expected Week of Confinement (EWC). The EWC commences on a Sunday at the start of the week in which the doctor or midwife estimates the baby will be born. This information will normally be given on Form MatB1. There is fortunately an easy way to determine the QW and this can be done from the tables produced annually by the DSS which set out all the QWs in a year related to the EWC. These tables are in leaflet SMP55 known as the *Red Book 3* and obtainable from your local DSS office.

Deciding which week is the qualifying week for SMP is one of the most important decisions necessitated by this scheme. Many of the other rules depend on events in that week, or in the weeks leading up to the qualifying week.

In further detail the qualifying conditions are as follows:

1. *Notice by employee.* The woman must give you at least 21 days' notice of her intention to leave work and start the Maternity Pay Period (MPP). The MPP is the 18 weeks maximum for which an employer can pay SMP. A woman cannot start the MPP earlier than the eleventh week before the EWC, which means that she would have to notify you no later than the end of the fifteenth week before the EWC. This rule can sometimes present the woman with great difficulties, particularly if the baby is born very early, or if she is on holiday and on her return decides that she is ready to give up work. Because of this employers are able to waive the 21 days' notice rule when it is accepted that it was not reasonably practicable for the employee to give the full 21 days' notice. This relaxation of the rule is entirely within the employer's discretion.

   If an employer decides not to pay SMP because the notice rule has not been complied with, then Form SMP1 (notice of exclusion) must be issued and the woman can then ask you for a written statement detailing why you cannot pay her the SMP. She may then ask the DSS to review the circumstances, and this may lead to an appeal by you or by the woman. Appeals are very often lengthy and sometimes expensive processes, and you may well consider that notice of intention to stop work of less than the 21 days, where there are fairly reasonable grounds, may not be sufficient reason to prevent you paying SMP.

2. *Continuous employment.* To satisfy this condition a woman needs to have been continuously employed by you for at least 26 weeks up to and including the qualifying week. She may not have worked for you every week, but the contract of employment should have been

in existence for that period. Once again booklet SMP55 shows the latest date for each qualifying week on which a woman should have started work with you. SMP weeks always start on Sunday, so for this rule to apply the woman's contract of employment must have been in existence on the Sunday that starts the twenty-sixth week before the QW. If she started work with you on the following Monday she does not fulfil this condition.

Where there has been a change of owner of a business, or the woman moves from one company to another within the same group, then this can be deemed to be continuous employment. Any doubt about this rule should be referred to your local DSS office.

3. *Average earnings rule.* A woman is entitled to the payment of SMP by her employer if her average earnings for an eight-week period are at a rate equal to or more than the lower earnings level for NIC. The eight-week period to be looked at is the eight weeks up to and including the last pay-day before the end of the qualifying week. The last day of the qualifying week is a Saturday, as all SMP weeks start on a Sunday, so that if the normal pay-day was Friday, it is the eight weeks ending with the Friday in the QW which must be looked at. This would normally give eight weeks' pay for weekly-paid people.

For fortnightly-paid people there would normally be four payments falling within the eight-week period, and these can be averaged out to give one week's pay. For monthly paid employees the last pay-day in or before the QW needs to be looked at, and thereafter the other payments falling in the eight weeks ending with that pay-day. This would normally give two monthly payments of salary, which should be added together, multiplied by 6 and then divided by 52 to give an average week's earnings. (This will not necessarily give the same result as dividing her current annual salary by 52.)

Where the pay interval has changed from weekly to monthly, or other irregular payments have been made in the eight-week period, employers need to look at the eight weeks ending with the last payment in or immediately before the QW. To do this, add together all the payments falling in that eight weeks, look at the period those payments were intended to cover (payments may have been made on the last day of two months and one odd week's earnings), divide the total payments by the number of days paid, and multiply that figure by 7 to obtain an average week's earnings. Appendix No 1 in leaflet NI257 gives some examples of these calculations.

The earnings which are to be taken into account are those which count for NIC purposes. This means that payment of holiday pay,

SSP, bonus, overtime or even a back-dated pay award covering a long period are included in the average earnings calculation. If a woman qualifies for the higher rate of SMP (see later in this chapter) then these additional payments can affect the amount she receives.

Because of the precise calculation which has to be made for each woman claiming SMP, this can mean that two employees working side by side on similar pay may have different SMP calculations and this can lead to queries put to the payroll office. It may well be that one woman has two weeks' holiday pay falling in the eight-week earnings period which will increase her average earnings, and therefore her entitlement to SMP. As with all calculations in a payroll office, full records need to be kept of precisely how payments are calculated so that the necessary explanations can be given to employees on pay-day.

These calculations may be more difficult at Christmas or other bank holiday times if normal wages are paid earlier than usual. At Easter, for example, weekly wages may be paid on Maundy Thursday instead of on Good Friday. In these circumstances it is the usual pay date that should be applied for the eight-week earnings rule. The calculation should be made as if the payments had been made on the right day and not specially moved forward for an event such as a bank holiday. Where the pay-day is moved by more than just a day or two, for example, salaries for 31 December paid before Christmas on 17 December, then employers can choose either to look back to the last *regular* payment (30 November) and count eight weeks up to that date, or treat the December salary as being paid on the proper date, and if this is then the last pay-day in or before the QW, count eight weeks up to that date.

4. *Evidence of Pregnancy.* The woman will normally give her employer Form MatB1 signed by her doctor or her midwife showing either the expected week of confinement or the actual date that the baby was born. Sometimes the doctor or midwife will only give the woman a letter, and in these circumstances you should make sure that the letter is properly signed; a midwife's letter should have her State Registered number. Employers should always keep the originals of these notifications and not return them to the woman if any payment of SMP is made. If the woman requires further evidence, for example for dental treatment, then she can get this from her doctor or midwife. The woman will normally bring the MatB1 to her employer when she wishes to give notice of the date on which she wants the maternity pay period to start. In the event of an early confinement, she may bring Form MatB1 in together with the baby!

5. *Ceasing work*. SMP cannot be paid for any period in which the woman works. SMP is always paid for whole weeks and can never be split up into days, so that any week in which a woman performs any work is excluded for SMP. This means that if a woman ceases work on the thirty-first day of the month and this falls on a Wednesday, she cannot receive any SMP until the following week, commencing on the Sunday. Moreover, if during the payment of SMP she returns to work, SMP cannot be paid for the week in which she returns. This is the case even if the woman is asked to come in for just an odd day to help out. Any work done, whether at home or unpaid, disqualifies her from the payment of SMP.

There are sometimes problems with women who have left your employment who have been receiving SMP for 18 weeks and who are not going to return to work with you. If the woman starts work for someone else after she has had the baby (unless she was also employed by them in the QW) then you must stop paying SMP.

These conditions are quite complicated, and because of this it is worth making sure that any relevant employees are aware of them, so that they can tell you if their circumstances change, for instance, if they start working for someone else.

Qualifying condition not satisfied
If any of the five qualifying conditions are not satisfied, then you should tell the employee as soon as possible that you will not be able to pay her SMP. This will give both of you an opportunity to check the facts before Form SMP1 is issued to the woman and her Form MatB1 returned to her. Even though an employer may be unable to pay SMP, the woman may be able to claim MA from the DSS. Once Form SMP1 has been issued to the woman, an employer should not pay SMP without informing the DSS.

Qualifying conditions satisfied
Once the qualifying conditions have been met, it is up to the employer to decide how much SMP to pay and from what date. The date on which the MPP is to start will normally be the week commencing Sunday following the three weeks' notice given by the woman. This date can never be earlier than the eleventh week before the EWC. If the woman wants to stay at work until closer to the birth of the baby she is free to do this, and it is up to her to choose on what date she wishes SMP to start. The MPP can start 11 weeks before the EWC, and must finish by the eleventh week after the EWC. Because of this the latest week that the woman should start to receive SMP is six weeks before the EWC so that she does not lose

entitlement to any of the 18 weeks payable. If she continues to work later than the sixth week before the EWC, then she can choose when the MPP can start, but it must finish at the eleventh week after the EWC. In these circumstances she will receive SMP for less than the 18 weeks maximum.

How much to pay

When an employer has decided that a woman fulfils all the qualifying conditions, then the amount of SMP payable needs to be decided. All women who qualify will be entitled to 18 weeks at a flat-rate weekly amount. This amount is notified to employers annually on leaflet SMP55, which sets out the table of dates etc, thus enabling employers to see at a glance the relevant dates and to calculate the correct amount of SMP owing.

There are, however, conditions under which the woman may be entitled to the higher rate of SMP. These conditions are as follows:

- if the woman has been continuously employed for two years up to and including the qualifying week, with at least sixteen hours worked weekly; *or*
- if the woman has been continuously employed for five years up to and including the qualifying week with at least eight but less than sixteen hours worked weekly.

There are similar rules for continuous employment as for the basic qualifying conditions. The woman's contract of employment with you should indicate the usual number of hours work required per week, but if this does not fulfil the 8- or 16-hour conditions, then you are able to consider whether overtime or extra hours were actually worked which would bring the woman within these conditions. If you neglect to give the woman the benefit of the doubt in these circumstances, and only pay her the basic rate of SMP, you may find that she will have five years' payslips which she will produce to you to show the actual hours she worked! You may recall that the Inland Revenue and the DSS require employers to keep records for three years only, and yet one of the requirements above needs five years' earnings history to be reviewed.

If a woman qualifies for the higher rate of SMP, this higher rate needs to be calculated for each individual. The higher rate is 90 per cent of the average earnings figure which was used for qualifying condition 3. If the woman's average earnings are inflated by a backdated pay award then the calculation will give an amount of SMP much larger than would have been expected. This is quite in order. Since the introduction of SMP, women have realised the potential of increasing the benefit, and occasionally work overtime or arrange for annual bonus payments to fall within the eight weeks used for the average earnings calculation.

The higher rate of SMP is not paid for the full 18 weeks' entitlement, and is limited to the first six weeks of payment. This is so even if the woman leaves work very late so that less than the maximum 18 weeks are payable.

An employer can to some extent choose how and when to pay SMP. A woman will sometimes ask for the whole of the 18 weeks' entitlement to be paid in one sum when she leaves employment. This, for various reasons, is not necessarily a good idea for either the woman or the employer, and the DSS prefer the final payment not to be made before it is due. Payments of SMP attract tax and NIC, and a very large payment in one week or month would normally result in maximum NI contributions from both the woman and the employer. Moreover, if the woman has already left employment and has been given her P45, then SMP would be a payment after leaving and should be taxed at the basic rate (repayment of any tax overpaid would be made by the tax office).

If, however, SMP is paid weekly or monthly in a similar way to the woman's pay before payment of SMP, then for NIC all payments of SMP at the flat rate will avoid any contribution at all from the employer or the employee, as these are below the lower earnings level. For tax purposes it is usually worthwhile for an employer to enquire of his tax office whether he may continue to use the normal code in operation, and not issue Form P45 until payment of SMP has been completed. This means that the woman receives the benefit of her tax-free pay each week or month, as payments are made.

Most employers find that payment of SMP is easily dealt with through the normal payroll system, so that when the SMP calculations have been done the amounts payable can be taxed and subjected to NI in the normal way. Any amount of SMP should be separately identified for payroll purposes, not only on the woman's payslip but also for the end-of-the-month totals, and end-of-year returns (see Chapters 14 and 15).

If SMP is processed through payroll, then it can be paid by cheque or Giro credit or BACS tape in the normal way, along with wages and salaries.

Although an employer may decide to pay SMP monthly, because this is a weekly benefit paid for whole weeks, it is a good idea not to split any weeks of payments into days. It is advisable for payroll to pay the four or five whole weeks that end in a monthly salary period.

Stopping payment of SMP

Employers should not forget that SMP is a short-term payment, and should remember to stop payment, at the latest when 18 weeks have been paid. There are other occasions when an employer will need to stop payment; these are as follows:

1. *Woman returns to work.* If a woman does any work at all during an SMP payment week then she cannot receive any SMP for the whole of that week. This means that if a woman leaves work 11 weeks before the baby is due, and comes back in the ninth week before EWC for one day's work, she loses entitlement to SMP for the whole of that week. If she is receiving SMP at the higher rate for six weeks, then she can still receive the full six weeks plus a reduced number of weeks at the flat rate.

   When the woman has had a baby, and she returns to work, even for a few days, she will normally lose her right to any further SMP. The problem arises when the woman starts work for an employer other than the one paying her SMP. An employer really needs to find this out, so that he may stop making any further payments. If you are paying SMP through payroll, and have not already issued Form P45, then it is possible the woman will come and ask for her P45, and this will give you an indication that she needs it because she has started work again. An employer cannot, of course, be held responsible for any overpayment of SMP where he was truly unaware that the woman's circumstances had changed. In all these matters the payroll office needs 'big ears', as it is likely that when the woman brings the baby in for her former colleagues to see, she may well mention that she is starting another job – if this is the case.

2. *Leaving the European Community.* If a woman leaves the EC at any time during the MPP, she loses her right to any further payments of SMP. Employees are normally quite good at following rules, once they know what they are, and in this instance it is worthwhile notifying employees that holidays in far-away places may prevent payment of SMP, so that trips abroad can be limited to EC countries. Should a woman then choose to leave the EC during the MPP, you should issue Form SMP1 as soon as possible.

3. *Woman taken into legal custody.* This is another occasion in which payroll needs to keep its eyes and ears open, as payment of SMP must stop. A woman loses her right to SMP from and including the week in which she is arrested. Legal custody means not being able to leave police custody and, as already mentioned, it is not the same thing as 'helping the police with their enquiries'.

4. *Woman dies.* Payment of SMP ceases from the end of the week in which the woman dies.

5. *Late or early birth.* The payment of SMP is not affected if the baby

is born late or if more than one baby is born. The maximum 18 weeks of SMP cannot be exceeded no matter how late the confinement.

If the baby is born early and SMP is already being paid, then again this does not affect the payments already calculated. If the baby is born before the MPP was due to start, then SMP is payable from the beginning of the week following that in which the baby was born.

If the baby is born before or during the qualifying week, the 26-week qualifying condition is deemed to be satisfied, provided the condition would have been satisfied but for the early confinement. In this case the period over which the earnings are averaged will be the eight weeks ending with the week before that in which the baby was born.

If the pregnancy ends other than by a live birth, and this is earlier than the 12-week before the EWC, no SMP is payable. The woman may be entitled to payments of SSP in these circumstances.

Statutory Sick Pay and how it affects SMP

SSP and SMP cannot be paid for the same week. If a woman is receiving SSP and her doctor says she is fit to return to work on, for example, Wednesday, if she then decides to start her MPP, payment of SMP cannot commence before the following Sunday.

A woman may be receiving occupational sick pay and SSP in the weeks before the baby is born, and if she remains sick, (and she may if she wishes) choose not to start the MPP at the eleventh week before the EWC. The employer has no right to transfer the woman from SSP to SMP at the eleventh week, but the transfer should be made at the sixth week before the EWC, so that the maximum 18 weeks of SMP can be paid.

Problems sometimes arise where a woman has been sick and then receives SMP, returns to work and goes sick again, particularly when she has in reality left the employment. The payroll and personnel departments together should ensure that a woman in these circumstances knows precisely when her contract of employment has ended, and that any payment of SMP through payroll, and the non-issue of Form P45 until the payment of SMP has finished, in no way affects that contract of employment. There have been cases where women have sought to have the contract of employment extended throughout the period of SMP, into a period of SSP, and have then asked for days of accrued holiday relating to these weeks.

Recovery of SMP

As with SSP, employers are operating the SMP scheme on behalf of the Government and are able to reclaim the whole amount of any SMP paid. As with SSP, employers are only entitled to reclaim amounts properly paid, and therefore any overpayments will usually be made good by the employer.

The reclaiming of SMP is done at the end of each tax month from the NI contributions that the employer has to pay over at that time. In addition, the employer is entitled to an amount of compensation that is broadly equal to the employer's NI contributions payable on SMP. The SMP compensation is currently 7.5 per cent (this changes from time to time), and the methods of reclaiming and dealing with this compensation are explained in Chapter 14.

Record-keeping

As with the statutory deductions of tax and NIC, care should be taken by employers to keep precise records of all relevant information and calculations relating to SMP. A record sheet is provided by the DSS (Form SMP2), and this details all the basic information that employers need to keep. The records need not be kept on this form, but if an employer decides to keep records in another form, for example on a computer, he should ensure that all the information on Form SMP2 is recorded. Form SMP2 will show the dates of the woman's maternity absence, and the dates and reasons for any weeks within the MPP for which SMP was not paid. It is a good idea to attach to this the calculation of the average earnings. This should be retained for at least three tax years following that in which SMP was paid, together with Form MatB1 or other evidence of the pregnancy. There must also be records of the SMP paid to each employee each month and end-of-year returns (see Chapters 14 and 15).

Errors

If an employer makes a mistake either in the record-keeping or in the calculation or dates of payment of SMP, then this must be corrected.

Payments already made should not be disturbed, but any overpayment or underpayment adjusted at the next payment date. If an employee has been excluded from SMP, and you discover that payment is due to be made, you should notify the DSS of this in case some state benefit has also been paid.

The position is more complicated when the error is discovered in the tax year following the one in which payments were made. You will need to write to the DSS and give details of the amounts actually paid, and the correct figures, and send a cheque to cover any SMP overpaid. If it is an underpayment then the amount owing should be paid to the woman at the first available opportunity.

Further advice

Employers should not attempt to pay any amounts of SMP without having *The Employer's Guide to SMP* (leaflet NI257) at their elbow, together with the current year's leaflet SMP55, the SMP tables known as *Red Book 3*. If there are still unresolved problems, then you should either contact your local DSS office or ring the freephone advice line for employers on 0800 393 539.

Part Four:
Documentation

12
PAYE Calendar

Introduction

The Pay As You Earn (PAYE) calendar, which applies for both tax and National Insurance (NI) purposes, starts on 6 April of each year and ends on the following 5 April of the next year. The year is divided up into weeks and months, and tax and NI tables are issued so that it is relatively easy for an employer to work out the correct calculations relevant to the pay intervals of his employees. Individuals are given tax allowances for a year, so that when all these allowances have been used up, the new year starts with a new set of allowances, notified to employers by a code for each employee.

Payroll offices are always exceptionally busy at each year-end, as apart from the reconciliations and return-making required at the end of the tax year, there is the preparation for the new tax year, and possible changes to NI rates and tax codes, etc, and in addition employees will still expect to get their normal weekly or monthly salary cheques on time.

The end of the year provides an ideal opportunity for payroll to check that the information which they hold for employees affecting tax and NI calculations and payments of Statutory Sick Pay (SSP) and Statutory Maternity Pay (SMP) is still correct. If there is to be an event during the year that will change any payment or deduction, then a note can be made at the start of the year so that these are not forgotten. Where, for example, an employee will reach the age of 16, or retirement age during the year this will affect NICs, and possibly pension contributions or payments. Certificates of election for certain married women and widows should be reviewed to make sure they are still valid and the qualifying conditions still fulfilled.

Part Four will deal with what to do at various times in the year and the actions required at the end of the year to comply with the Inland Revenue and DSS requirements.

117

Information-gathering

The function of payroll can be said to be the timely and accurate payment of salaries or wages in accordance with the contract of employment. If a payroll office is going to perform this function both promptly and accurately, it needs to make sure that the information it receives can be verified as correct, and is received early enough to process the payroll so that payments are made to employees on time. The larger the organisation, obviously the more difficult this task becomes. A business with four employees can normally be expected to know that they were all at work all week, and it is a relatively simple task to record what hours were worked. Once the management or control of the business is divided between several people, then there will be a number of different people reporting information for payroll purposes.

A real problem for any large organisation – and one that needs to be stressed – is verification of payroll data. It is normal for the signatures of authorised persons to be kept in the payroll office, and overtime and bonus reports, etc can be checked against these to confirm the signature of the authorised person. This is a relatively easy system to monitor, but it can go awry in two ways: first when the authorising person is on holiday and an unauthorised deputy completes the work returns. It takes time for payroll to obtain the necessary authorisation – and time is something that a payroll office is always short of. This lack of time creates the second problem, if overtime or other work returns are received at the last minute, then a decision has to be made whether to leave the overtime out for that week because it is not properly authorised, or to pay the amounts shown with 'fingers crossed'. Most payroll offices will take the latter action, as they know that non-payment of overtime or bonus will result in a telephone call or personal visit by every person concerned, probably on Friday afternoon.

How much information is needed?

It is all very well having an authorised and timely system, but how do payroll monitor whether they have received all the information they should have received? For instance, if there are multiple work areas and returns, in a large organisation, would the payroll office be certain whether there should be 20 or 21 returns in a particular section in the week? The 21 wages sheets may have left the section, and only 20 be delivered because one has, perhaps, blown off the top of the pile. This problem is very easy to correct. It is usually possible to ask authorising personnel to complete a 'top sheet' for each batch of work returns, showing the week ending, the number of sheets enclosed, and the total of hours and overtime, etc worked on the enclosed returns. It is then a simple matter for payroll to count the number of sheets received and tally the hours with the information given.

Deadlines

Payroll offices need to carry out a 'critical path analysis', and this is done without most people being aware of the technical term. This simply means that when the time of payment of salary or wages is known, the times for various payroll functions can be set and deadlines imposed. For example, let us suppose that salaries are to be credited to bank accounts on the last day of the month: the bank may require 36 hours notice, the payroll manager may want to carry out certain checks after the payroll run has been done. Consequently, basic information, such as overtime returns, must be received in the payroll office by certain set time limits, in order to allow time for authorisation and processing.

These deadlines have to be workable from everyone's point of view. It is no good telling a workshop that the returns for a week ending at 5 pm on Friday must be with payroll by 8 am on Monday, particularly if they are separated by any distance. If the geographical location of the sites involved is too great, then overtime or bonus could be paid a week in arrears. It is advisable to seek agreement on deadlines between the parties involved, and once agreement has been reached it should be adhered to as far as possible. If the payroll office allows a relaxation of the deadlines on every occasion, then the individual on whom the deadline is imposed will probably not take it seriously.

Interaction with the personnel department

Most larger organisations these days have separate personnel and payroll functions headed by a payroll manager and a personnel manager. There can be problems with two separate departments, particularly when the lines of communication between them are less than perfect. The personnel function is concerned with the preparation of contracts of employment, hiring the right candidate and occasionally firing the wrong one. In between there are all sorts of problems relating to sickness or injury at work, unsatisfactory work or personal problems. Payroll, on the other hand, is normally concerned with things of a more exact nature, such as finite amounts of salary, commission, etc which affect a known number of people at a set time. It is true to say that most personnel people have no idea how a payroll department runs, or of the complications inherent in the tax, NI, SSP and SMP systems. Because of this they are not always aware of the necessity for receiving fast and accurate information. However it is done, the payroll department must try to ensure that all the people they rely on for information know exactly what information is needed and when it is wanted.

With the growth in computerised payrolls it is evident that much of the information about employees is common to both the payroll and personnel departments, and many companies both large and small have combined the two functions. In the firms where this has taken place there do not seem to have been great problems, but it is true to say that on many occasions the pay of payroll staff has had to be upgraded to that of their personnel colleagues!

13
What to Do on Pay-Day

Gross pay

Most payroll departments have, in advance of pay-day, established the total amount of payments to be made to employees. The gross pay will include normal wages or salary, together with any bonus or overtime and also any amount of occupational sick pay and Statutory Sick Pay (SSP) or occupational maternity pay or Statutory Maternity Pay (SMP). In addition, gross pay will include round sum expenses or any identifiable part of expenses that gives a profit element.

Tax-free payments

To secure the right employee for the job, during the interview you may have agreed to pay the right candidate's salary free of tax. However, this is not as simple as it sounds. For example, if an employee is to receive a salary of, say, £12,000 per annum and the tax he is to pay amounts to £2000, his net pay would be £10,000 per annum. Where, however, the employer pays the £2000 tax on his employee's behalf, this is seen as a taxable emolument to the employee, in other words, it is a taxable sum of money in itself. So, the tax on the tax of £2000 would amount to, say, £500 but again, this is seen as a further emolument on which tax is due, and on it goes until it is reduced to nothing. This means that for a payment to be truly tax-free, a gross figure has to be worked out which, after the proper tax deductions, will leave the employee with the agreed figure. In the above instance, about £13,500 would need to be paid to result in a net payment of £10,000 after tax deductions. Employers can do this calculation on a hit-or-miss basis, or ask their local tax office for a leaflet FOT1 and 'free of tax' tables, tables G. There is an additional special deductions working sheet P11FOT.

Tax-free sums of money are most likely to be paid in special

121

circumstances. For example, in the event of employees' conditions of work being changed, a lump sum is sometimes paid 'free of tax' in order to soften the blow, but this will need to be 'grossed up' before the net amount is paid to the employees.

Week 53, 54 or 56 payments

There are normally 52 weeks in a tax year, but as there are 365 days, and 366 in a leap year, this actually amounts to 52 weeks and one or two extra days. Where wages are paid regularly on a Friday it will happen once every few years that the Friday of payment will be 4 or 5 April, and yet the 52 weeks of the tax year will already have been used up. When this happens an extra week's payment, called a week 53 payment, is inserted. Where payments are made fortnightly and the tax tables have been used on weeks 2, 4, 6, 8, etc, then this extra payment will need to be a week 54 payment. Similarly, with four-weekly pay, normally 13 four-weekly payments will be made in a year, so that the last normal payment will be made in week 52 of the tax tables. Where the last payment of the year falls on 4 or 5 April and week 52 has already been used, then the final payment of the year will be a week 56 payment.

There is an extra line for this payment below week 52 on Form P11 (deductions working sheet), and the pay for the week should be entered in here with tax deducted as if it were week 1 of the tax year. This means that the free pay for week 1 needs to be deducted from the pay for the week, to calculate the taxable pay and the tax due. This final payment can then be added into the totals of pay and tax deducted for the year (week 2 and week 4 tables will be used for weeks 54 or 56 respectively).

Deductions

Deductions from gross pay can be separated into statutory and non-statutory items. Normally the first item to be considered is the pension contribution, assuming you have an approved pension scheme for employees, so an amount needs to be deducted from the pay of each employee concerned and the total contributions sent to the pension provider, eg the insurance company, each month. The amount of the deduction would normally be a percentage of an employee's basic salary, but may also be a percentage of extra payments such as overtime or commission. This will depend upon the rules of the pension scheme. The pension contribution is deducted from the amount of money the employee will receive, and approved contributions are deducted before income tax is calculated. National Insurance contributions (NICs) are, however, calculated on the gross before pension contributions are deducted.

In a similar way, 'Give As You Earn' can be deducted from gross pay before tax is calculated, but not for NIC. This will only apply where an employer has an approved charity-giving scheme.

Tax and NIC are both deductions from pay in arriving at the net pay to employees. If you are in any doubt as to which of these statutory deductions to take first, both departments will tell you that theirs is the primary deduction. You will, however, normally have enough pay to satisfy both departments at once.

From time to time the payroll office may receive instructions from a court to deduct amounts due under a court order from an employee's pay and send the money deducted to the court each week or month. You will receive precise instructions about this, and you should also note that a business is allowed to charge a fee for providing this service, which can be deducted from the amount payable to the court.

Other deductions

The payroll office will often be asked to collect various amounts from an employee's pay, such as subscriptions to the company's sports and social club, or to a savings or holiday club. These deductions (authorised by the employees in writing) will be made after tax and NIC deductions, and the total amounts deducted each week or month will need to be transferred to the fund-holder.

Weekly or monthly pay?

If as an employer you have a choice whether to pay salaries on a weekly or monthly basis, or at some other interval, then the best decision is to pay your employees on a monthly basis. The simple reason for this is that the calculation of all the statutory deductions will take the same amount of time whether they are computed on a week's pay or a month's salary. If these calculations take, say, an hour per person, then for weekly staff this is 52 hours in a year and for monthly paid staff only 12 hours. Monthly payments also give the payroll officer more time to obtain all the information he or she needs, and also to make the necessary complicated calculations.

Deductions working sheet (Form P11)

For each employee for whom you are to calculate net pay it is necessary to prepare a deductions working sheet Form P11. There are many payroll systems on the market, both manual and computerised, but you will find the information on them is similar to that required on the Inland

Deductions Working Sheet P11(87) Year to 5 April 19

Employer's name

GREENTREES LTD

Tax District and reference

ANYTOWN   P123 / 6789

Complete only for occupational pension schemes newly contracted-out since 1 January 1986.
Scheme contracted-out number

S	4						

National Insurance Contributions *

Earnings on which employee's contributions payable 1a	Total of employee's and employer's contributions payable 1b	Employee's contributions payable 1c	Earnings on which employee's contributions at contracted-out rate payable included in column 1a 1d	Employee's contributions at contracted-out rate included in column 1c 1e	Statutory Sick Pay in the week or month included in column 2 1f	Statutory Maternity Pay in the week or month included in column 2 1g	Month no
'A' 176	34 32	15 88	£	·	£	£	6 April to 5 May 1
'D' 184	27 67	13 77	141	9 90			
							6 May to 5 June 2
							6 June to 5 July 3
							6 July to 5 Aug 4
							6 Aug to 5 Sept 5
							6 Sept to 5 Oct 6
							6 Oct to 5 Nov 7
Total c/forward	Total c/forward	Total c/forward	Total c/forward	Total c/forward	Total c/forward	Total c/forward	

P11(87)

PRINTED IN THE UK FOR HMSO BY COLIBRI PRESS LTD   11/86 Dd 8875918

Employee's surname *in CAPITALS*					First two forenames		
MACLEAN					HELEN JENNY		

National Insurance no.		Date of birth *in figures*			Works no. etc	Date of leaving *in figures*	
YA , 03 , 05 , 11 , B		Day 4	Month 12	Year 61		Day Month Year	

Tax code †	Amended code †				
278L	Wk/Mth in which applied				

PAYE Income Tax

Week no	Pay in the week or month including Statutory Sick Pay/ Statutory Maternity Pay 2	Total pay to date 3	Total free pay to date as shown by Table A 4	Total taxable pay to date Ø 5	Total tax due to date as shown by Taxable Pay Tables 6	Tax deducted or refunded in the week or month *Mark refunds 'R'* 7	For employer's use
1	176 50	176 50	53 64	122 86	30 50	30 50	
2	184 70	361 20	107 28	253 92	63 25	32 75	
3							
4							
5							
6							
7							
8							
9							
10							
11							
12							
13							
14							
15							
16							
17							
18							
19							
20							
21							
22							
23							
24							
25							
26							
27							
28							
29							
30							

* You must enter the NI contribution table letter overleaf beside the NI totals box - *see the note shown there.*

† If amended cross out previous code.

Ø If in any week/month the amount in column 4 is more than the amount in column 3, leave column 5 blank.

Figure 13.1 *Deductions working sheet*

Source: Inland Revenue, P11(87)

Revenue's Form P11. The left-hand side of Form P11 is connected with NIC, Statutory Sick Pay (SSP) and Statutory Maternity Pay (SMP). The right-hand side of the form is concerned with income tax. The first step is to complete the top of the form with the employer's name and address and tax district, and the employee's surname and other details, including the tax code applicable to that individual employee. A new Form P11 is prepared for each new tax year, starting on 6 April, and the first pay-day that falls on or after 6 April will normally be week 1 for weekly paid people or month 1 for monthly paid people.

Calculation of NIC

Columns 1a to 1e of Form P11 are concerned with NIC. The amounts to be entered in these columns are copied from the amounts shown in the NIC tables. The appropriate table will have been determined for each employee and the category letter, for example A, B, C or D, can be entered in the margin as a reminder for each week or month. For not contracted-out contributions, columns 1a–1c will be completed. But, in addition, for contracted-out contributions, columns 1d and 1e will also be completed. If an employee joins the approved pension scheme, then his category of NIC will change and this will be noted on the P11 (see Figure 13.1). Columns 1f and 1g can be used to record the amounts of SSP and SMP to be paid in that week or month, which are to be included in gross pay for both NI and tax purposes.

Calculating income tax

At the beginning of each tax year the first payment of salary or wages will normally be made in week 1 or month 1 of the tax year. It is the date of payment which governs which week or tax month is to be used, and the dates covered by each tax period are shown for easy reference at the top of each page on the tax tables. For a new employee, the first week's or month's pay will be entered on Form P11 in the appropriate tax period, not necessarily week 1 or month 1 of the tax year.

Gross pay for tax purposes is entered in column 2 of Form P11 and the total pay to date entered in column 3. This means that for the first pay period in the year the total pay to date will be the same as the pay in that week or month, but for subsequent pay-days will indicate the total taxable pay for the year, and this could be from previous employments not just the employment with you. Column 4 of Form P11 is headed 'Total free pay to date as shown by table A'. The free pay is obtained by looking up the tax code in the free-pay tables for the relevant week or month. The figure

TABLE B

LIMITATIONS ON USE

	Pay at Weekly rates				Pay at Monthly rates	
Week No.	If total taxable pay to date does not exceed	Total tax due to date		Month No.	If total taxable pay to date does not exceed	Total tax due to date
	Col. 1 £	Col. 2 £			Col. 1 £	Col. 2 £
1	399			1	1725	
2	797			2	3450	
3	1195			3	5175	TAX DUE AS SHOWN IN TABLE B
4	1593			4	6900	If the total taxable pay exceeds the figure in Col. 1 refer to Table C as appropriate
5	1991			5	8625	
6	2389			6	10350	
7	2787			7	12075	
8	3185			8	13800	
9	3583			9	15525	
10	3981			10	17250	
11	4379			11	18975	
12	4777			12	20700	
13	5175					
14	5574					
15	5972					
16	6370					
17	6768					
18	7166					
19	7564					
20	7962					
21	8360					
22	8758	TAX DUE AS SHOWN IN TABLE B				
23	9156	If the total taxable pay exceeds the figure in Col. 1 refer to Table C as appropriate				
24	9554					
25	9952					
26	10350					
27	10749					
28	11147					
29	11545					
30	11943					
31	12341					
32	12739					
33	13137					
34	13535					
35	13933					
36	14331					
37	14729					
38	15127					
39	15525					
40	15924					
41	16322					
42	16720					
43	17118					
44	17516					
45	17914					
46	18312					
47	18710					
48	19108					
49	19506					
50	19904					
51	20302					
52	20700					

Table 13.1 *Table B: Limitations on use*

Source: Inland Revenue

in column 5 is obtained by subtracting free pay in column 4 from total pay to date in column 3. Having established taxable pay, this figure is looked up in the taxable-pay tables to give the total tax due to date for entry in column 6. The tax deducted or refunded in the week or month to be entered in column 7 in the first pay period of the year will be the figure in column 6, but the subsequent pay-days will be the last entry in column 6 less the previous pay period's entry.

This sounds – and is – complicated, but after two or three repetitions it will become second nature. The example shown in Figure 13.2 gives the first four weeks of the tax year and it would be a good idea to follow these through, so that the sequence of use of tables, etc is grasped.

Higher-rate taxpayers

There are currently two rate bands for income tax for individuals: 25 per cent and 40 per cent. Only the first band of income is taxable at 25 per cent and this band, known as the basic rate band, is spread over the tax year by the tax tables. This means that if an employee were to earn an exceptional amount of pay in the early weeks of the tax year because, for example, he has an annual amount of bonus added to his normal salary, then this may distort his earnings pattern so that if he were to continue to receive pay at that rate regularly, he would be liable for higher-rate tax, whereas when on normal pay he would not be. In order that the correct amount of tax is deducted, the tax tables are issued with a 'limitations on use' chart, normally on page 3 of the taxable pay tables (see Table 13.1). This means that for each pay period the taxable pay should be compared with this figure: if it exceeds it, then the special system detailed on that chart should be followed. This means that higher-rate tax will be deducted in that week or month.

What to do if an employee starts part way through a year

You will remember from Chapter 5 that employees are of two kinds: those with Form P45 and those without. For employees with Form P45, Form P11 will need to be completed as shown in Figure 13.2.

Week 1 basis
An employee who arrives without Form P45 will normally have his tax calculated on a week 1 basis, often on the emergency code. At any time during the tax year the tax office can instruct you to operate a code on a 'week 1 or month 1 basis'. Entries on Form P11 should be as shown in Figure 13.3.

Employee's surname *in CAPITALS* SIMMONDS		First two forenames DAVID GORDON		
National Insurance no. ZL 21 04 11 C	Date of birth *in figures* Day 11 Month 6 Year 59	Works no. etc		Date of leaving *in figures* Day Month Year

Tax code † 437H	Amended code † Wk/Mth in which applied	456H WK4		

PAYE Income Tax

Week no	Pay in the week or month including Statutory Sick Pay/ Statutory Maternity Pay 2	Total pay to date 3	Total free pay to date as shown by Table A 4	Total taxable pay to date Ø 5	Total tax due to date as shown by Taxable Pay Tables 6	Tax deducted or refunded in the week or month Mark refunds 'R' 7	For employer's use
1	275 25	275 25	84 22	191 03	47 75	47 75	
2	264 50	539 75	168 44	371 31	92 75	45 00	
3	165 90	705 65	252 66	452 99	113 00	20 25	
4	210 70	916 35	351 48	564 87	141 00	28 00	
5							
6							
7							
8							
9							
10							
11							
12							
13							
14							
15							
16							
17							
18							
19							
20							
21							
22							
23							
24							
25							
26							
27							
28							
29							
30							

* You must enter the NI contribution table letter overleaf beside the NI totals box - *see the note shown there.*

† If amended cross out previous code.

Ø If in any week/month the amount in column 4 is more than the amount in column 3, leave column 5 blank.

Figure 13.2 *Taxable pay form*

Source: Inland Revenue, P11

Employee's surname *in CAPITALS*		First two forenames		
SUTHERLAND		JENNY SUE		

National Insurance no.	Date of birth *in figures*	Works no. etc	Date of leaving *in figures*
YM, 15, 25, 10, D	Day 21, Month 04, Year 55		Day, Month, Year

Tax code †	Amended code †				
278L	Wk/Mth in which applied				

PAYE Income Tax

Week no	Pay in the week or month including Statutory Sick Pay/ Statutory Maternity Pay 2	Total pay to date 3	Total free pay to date as shown by Table A 4	Total taxable pay to date Ø 5	Total tax due to date as shown by Taxable Pay Tables 6	Tax deducted or refunded in the week or month *Mark refunds 'R'* 7	For employer's use
	£	£	£	£	£	£	
1							
2							
3							
4							
5							
6							
7							
8	195 50		53 64	141 86		35 25	
9	211 65		53 64	158 01		39 50	
10	208 90		53 64	155 26		38 75	
11							
12							
13							
14							
15							
16							
17							
18							
19							
20							
21							
22							
23							
24							
25							
26							
27							
28							
29							
30							

* You must enter the NI contribution table letter overleaf beside the NI totals box - *see the note shown there.*

† If amended cross out previous code.

Ø If in any week/month the amount in column 4 is more than the amount in column 3, leave column 5 blank.

Figure 13.3 *Tax pay form P11*

Source: Inland Revenue, P11

Dealing with errors

From time to time in any busy office errors are bound to occur. If these are a matter of a simple mistake in looking up a figure, then the incorrect amount can be crossed through lightly, and the correct figure and any adjustments necessary can be made above the original figures. It is an accepted fact in a payroll office that if you underpay an employee by any amount, the phone will ring approximately five seconds after receipt of the payslip, but any overpayments to employees tend to be met by silence. If an employee is overpaid because insufficient tax or NIC deductions have been made, then it may not always be possible to reclaim the amounts overpaid from the employees. The recovery will depend on whether the error was one of fact or law, and there have been a number of court cases relative to this. Employers are advised to notify an employee as soon as an error is discovered and where it is substantial seek agreement on when and how the amount of overpayment is to be recovered. Agreement to a recovery should be formalised in a letter from the payroll office to the employee.

Payslips and methods of payment

Employees will expect to receive a payslip detailing how the net pay that has arrived in their bank account has been calculated. Payslips can be bought from stationers ready made and many of the payroll systems that can be bought, including computerised ones, will supply a selection of payslips or you can prepare your own.

An employer is required by law to prepare a payslip showing various items. It is, however, sound practice to detail each and every item that has been included in the calculation of gross pay, and each deduction in computing net pay.

For example, payslips should have the following noted at the top of each slip:

- the company's name;
- the name of the employee;
- the applicable tax week or month;
- the employee's tax code;
- gross pay for the period;
- method of payment.

Leaving an appropriate space, the following information should be noted:

- gross pay for tax purposes;
- gross taxable pay to date;

- tax due to date;
- tax refund (if any, the amount is usually noted with 'R' beside it);
- the tax deducted from this week/month;
- employee's NI deductions;
- SSP or SMP.

Any other deductions, ie for pension etc, should be noted here.

The last item on a payslip shows the total deduction figure taken from the employee's salary. Below this figure, in a separate section, should be noted the employer's NI and pension contributions (if any).

Since the repeal of the Truck Acts employers can no longer be required to make payments of wages in cash. Where, however, there are still contracts of employment in existence which say that payment will be made in cash, then these have to be continued unless the terms of the contract can be varied by mutual agreement. The UK is one of the few countries left in Europe who still pay employees in cash, and it can be hard to understand that this factor is still an important one in pay negotiations. Any new employer should ensure that his company's contracts of employment stipulate that payment of wages or salary will be made other than by cash.

There are a number of reasons for not paying by cash, and security is one of the foremost. The arrangements necessary to ensure that cash is secure while in transit to and from your premises are expensive and can carry a risk to life. Expense is also incurred through the additional manpower needed to count and make up cash into wage packets.

The simplest alternative to paying by cash is for a cheque to be prepared for each employee which he can then bank. However, this may well not be practicable for more than a handful of employees who are used to cash payments, they may want to take time off during working hours to bank their cheques.

Bank giro credit can be arranged through the company's bankers, so that amounts will be credited to employees' bank accounts on the appointed day. Employers of large numbers of staff, particularly those with computer systems for payroll, will normally pay by the 'BACS' system and really 'hi-tech user friendly' systems can do this using a telephone line.

14

Actions to be Taken at the End of Each Month

A tax month will always end on the fifth day of the month in question, having started on the sixth day of the previous month. This means that you will normally have made one monthly salary payment, often on the last day of the calendar month, or four or five weekly payments. The end of the month procedures do not in any way affect the tax and National Insurance (NI) calculations you make for employees, but are additional procedures.

You are required to send to the Inland Revenue accounts office, within 14 days of the end of a tax month, the total of all the tax and NIC deducted in the month, less any payments of SSP or SMP and the NIC compensation. You will be provided with a payslip booklet by the Inland Revenue accounts office when you first become an employer, and at the start of each year, and this will normally contain payslips for 12 payments to be made in the year. The first pages of the booklet are divided up into columns so that the totals of tax, NIC etc for each month can be itemised. This is an opportunity for employers to balance their books at the end of each month, and any small errors that have occurred will normally be highlighted at this time. The booklet gives instructions on how the net payment to the Accounts Office is calculated and the record of this is kept in the booklet, (see Figure 14.1). One of the 12 Inland Revenue payslips, should be completed and sent to the Accounts Office with your payment by the nineteenth day of each month (see Figure 14.2).

Very rarely, an employer will have paid out more in SSP and SMP than he has deducted in tax and NI, and in these circumstances he is instructed either to deduct the excess from the next month's payment, or, if he cannot do this, to write to the Accounts Office and explain his figures and ask for a cheque for the money for which he is out of pocket. This situation is only likely to occur in an unusual instance, eg in the case of an epidemic of Asian Flu or similar virus affecting many employees.

Record of deductions from gross National Insurance

Period ending	1 Statutory Sick Pay (SSP) £	2 NIC Compensation on SSP £	3 Statutory Maternity Pay (SMP) £	4 NIC Compensation on SMP £	5 Total deductions Total of 1, 2, 3 and 4. Carry forward to col. 3, page 5 £
5 May	88 35	6 63	145 00	10 88	250 86
5 Jun					
5 Jul					
5 Aug					
5 Sep					
5 Oct					
5 Nov					
5 Dec					
5 Jan					
5 Feb					
5 Mar					
5 Apr					
Total					

Record of Payments

Period ending	1 Income Tax £		2 Gross National Insurance £		3 Total deductions *Amount from col. 5, page 4* £		4 Net National Insurance *(2 less 3)* £		5 Total amount due *(1+4)* £		Date paid
5 May	2045	25	1486	27	250	86	1235	41	3280	66	19/5
5 Jun											
5 Jul											
5 Aug											
5 Sep											
5 Oct											
5 Nov											
5 Dec											
5 Jan											
5 Feb											
5 Mar											
5 Apr											
Total											

Page 5

You are advised to complete the above record each time you make a payment. This information will be required when you complete the Employer's Annual Statement, Declaration and Certificate

Figure 14.1 *Working sheet for income tax and NI deductions*

Source: Inland Revenue, P30B(2)

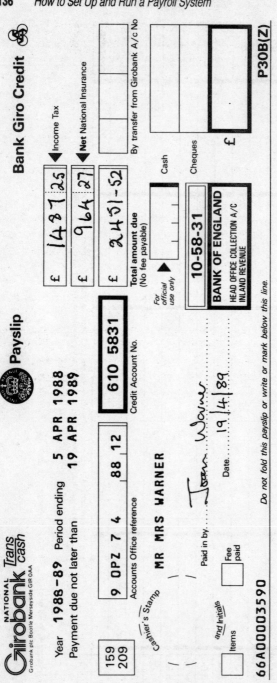

Figure 14.2 Inland Revenue payslip

Source: Inland Revenue, P(30)B2

The monthly payments should be sent to the Accounts Office by a specified date, ie the nineteenth day of each month. If an employer is late in sending this payment, he may receive a visit from the Collector's audit staff who may want to look at the payroll records. Employers with a large payroll may find that they have a visit from the local Collector's office every month in order to collect the cheque, once an arrangement has been made for this.

The accounts office is concerned that it has received, after the end of each month, the correct amount of tax and NIC, less any proper deductions. An employer should be concerned that the net amount he has paid out in wages and salary from the bank does also reflect the figures on the deductions working sheets or other pay records. The net wages or salary paid to an employee is not shown on the deductions working sheet, and employers normally have a wages summary book in which the net payments to employees are reconciled. There is an opportunity at the end of each tax month for an employer to carry out his own internal checks as well as those relating to income tax and NIC. A word of warning! There is always opportunity for simple theft or even fraud in a payroll office, as there is in any other department which deals with money. Even where cash is not handled it has been known for 'ghost' employees to be created and their pay diverted into the bank account of another employee. The firm's auditors will normally check for this kind of practice at the time of the firm's annual audit or when the company's accounts are prepared.

15

Actions to be Taken at the End of the Tax Year

The tax year ends on 5 April each year and shortly after that date all employers are required to make returns in respect of all individuals that they have employed at any time throughout the year, together with summaries of their pay, tax deductions, National Insurance Contributions (NIC) and any Statutory Sick Pay (SSP) and Statutory Maternity Pay (SMP) paid. At the end of each month employers will have sent a payslip with a cheque to the Inland Revenue Accounts Office, but normally there will have been no reconciliation during the year by the Collector to verify the amounts received. After the end of the tax year the tax and NI, etc for each employee are totalled and these totals should equal the sum of the 12 monthly payments sent to the Collector.

This is where the advantages of an employer balancing the books each month when the remittances are sent will be apparent. If this has been done, then the reconciliation of tax and NIC, etc at the end of the year should present no problems.

Apart from reconciling the statutory deductions, the Inspector of Taxes will need to know the precise amounts of pay and tax deducted for each of your employees during the year, and the Department of Social Security (DSS) will want to know the amount of NIC paid, and in what category, for each employee, together with the amount of the employer's contribution. This means that a separate return has to be sent in for *each* individual employee to both the Inland Revenue and DSS; fortunately both departments get a copy of the same form. The procedures involve the payroll department in a lot of extra work, often at the time of Easter holidays, and in addition the normal weekly or monthly salaries will need to be paid as usual. The current time limit for employers to submit all the required returns is 19 April, 14 days after the end of the tax year, but from 1990, this deadline is extended to 19 May.

Unfortunately, although employers will have an extra month to make these financial returns, there will be automatic penalties for returns made late. The penalties will be phased in, coming into force in May 1995, and are outlined in the 1989 Finance Act.

Employee Return Form P14

Form P14 has to be completed for each employee who you have employed at any time during the year, not just those who are with you at the end of the year. All the pay records throughout the year need to be examined and the totals extracted. A supply of Forms P14 will be sent to you by the tax office at the end of each year, together with the other end-of-year returns required. If you need further supplies, these can be obtained from your tax office. Many large firms who use a computer payroll will have continuous stationery P14s, so that these can be printed automatically. The form is produced in three parts, one for the tax office, one for the DSS and the bottom being the Form P60, certificate of pay and tax deducted for employees (see page 142).

The items for P14 are the employee's full name, including Christian names where known, and home address if possible, together with the employee's NI number. This number is particularly important as both the Inland Revenue and the DSS use it to trace employees on their own computers. There are boxes on the form for the total pay in the year, and the tax deducted or refunded, and separate boxes for details of pay and tax from your firm, and from any previous employment notified to you on Form P45 when the employee commenced work with you. NIC contributions (in your employment only) are shown by category and the totals for each of the columns on Form P11 must be shown. The employee's tax code at the end of the year is entered, and there are boxes for any payments made and tax deducted in week 53. Employers are also required to indicate if the employee is a director or pensioner and, if the employee left during the year, the date of leaving.

If an employer chooses to use any method of making these returns other than the P14 issued by the tax office, then he must make sure that all the information contained on the official P14 is included in his substitute returns. This is particularly true where information is sent in on 'floppy disk' or 'magnetic tape'. If you wish to use these facilities, you must obtain permission in advance from both government departments concerned. An illustration of a completed Form P14 is shown in Figure 15.1. An employer should not forget to fill in his own name and address, tax district and reference number, in addition to all the information about the employee.

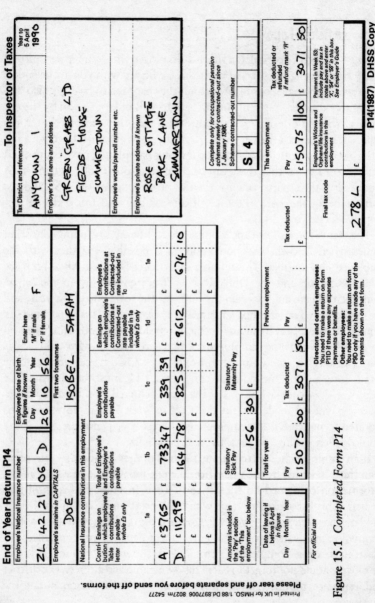

Figure 15.1 *Completed Form P14*

Source: Department of Social Security, P14

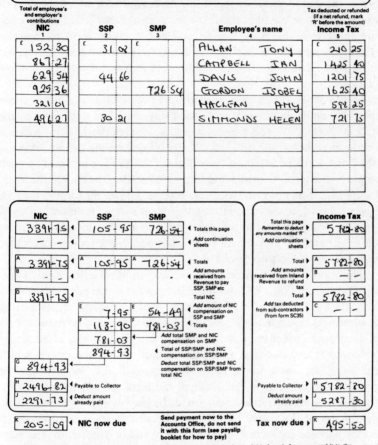

Figure 15.2 *1988/89 Deduction working sheets*

Source: Inland Revenue, P35

Employer's Return Form P35

The employer's return form is entitled 'Employers Annual Statement, Declaration and Certificate'. The front of the form has to be signed in person by the employer making the declaration and should not be stamped with the company's name and address. The form is sent to employers before the end of the year, together with Form P35X which explains to some extent how the form should be completed. Form P35 is to be sent to the Inspector of Taxes by 19 April, together with the top two copies of Form P14. As with Forms P14, this date is to be extended to 19 May, but automatic penalties for late returns are to be introduced over the next few years.

Form P35 is a summary of all Forms P14 completed, and continuation sheets are available where there are too many employees to be listed on the back of Form P35. The information to be entered on the form for each employee is their name, total of tax and NI deductions and any SSP and SMP paid to individual employees during the year. The amounts for each employee are totalled up and that figure is entered on the back of the form. Figure 15.2 shows how the totals are processed down the form so that the payments made to the Inland Revenue Accounts Office for months 1 to 11 are deducted from the totals for the year, leaving the month 12 payment shown separately. This should be an additional check for employers that they have balanced their books.

The month 12 payment must be sent to the Collector of Taxes separately from Form P35, with the last payslip in the payslip booklet.

At the back of Form P35 is the summary of the cash payments relating to employees throughout the year. The front of Form P35 contains a series of questions to which employers are required to give answers. These should be looked at very carefully, as they are an indication of the areas in which employers are most likely to have operated PAYE incorrectly. The declarations on the right-hand side of the form are concerned with the completeness of the returns being made by the employer and leave little room for error (see Figure 15.3). This is because there are penalties which can be imposed for incorrect completion of end-of-year returns (see page 148).

Employer's Return Form P38A

Question 1 on the front of Form P35 relates to casual employees for whom a Form P14 has not been prepared. You will need to list the names and addresses and amounts paid to these people on Form P38A and submit this with Form P35.

Inland Revenue
PAYE, National Insurance contributions
Statutory Sick Pay and
Statutory Maternity Pay

Accounts Office reference
9 1 0 P Z 5 2 7 8 9

Employers annual statement, declaration and certificate: 6 April 1988 to 5 April 1989

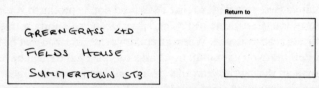

GREENGRASS LTD
FIELDS HOUSE
SUMMERTOWN ST3

Return to

You are required to
- make an End of Year Return on form P14 for each employee for whom you were required to complete a Deductions Working Sheet during the year **and**
- complete this form, sign the declaration and certificate and return it, together with the completed End of Year Returns, **by 19 April 1989.**

The enclosed leaflet P35X will help you to complete this form.

Questions
Please answer each question 'Yes' or 'No'

1 During the year 1988-89 did you make payments to any person employed by you, either on a casual basis or otherwise, for whom you have not enclosed an End of Year Return (form P14)?

If the answer is 'Yes', please give details on form P38A for any person who is within the categories described on that form.

Answer **YES**

2 Did you agree to bear any of the tax liability of any of your employees?

Answer **NO**

3 Did you, for 30 consecutive days or more, have the services in the UK of any individual employed by a person outside the UK and who is not included in the list on the back of this form or on any continuation sheets?

Answer **NO**

4 Did any other person, to your knowledge -
- pay expenses,
- provide benefits or
- award vouchers exchangeable for money, goods or services

to any of your employees because they were employed by you during the period?

Answer **NO**

5 Have you paid part or all of the pay of an employee to someone other than that employee (for example, to a school) which has not been included in the payments shown on the employee's End of Year Return (form P14)?

Answer **NO**

Declaration and certificate
False statements may result in prosecution or penalties

This declaration and certificate covers any documents prepared by me which have been authorised by the Commissioners of Inland Revenue as End of Year Returns.

I declare and certify that for the year 1988-89 -
- I enclose all the End of Year Returns (forms P14) which I am required to complete
- completed forms P11D and/or form P11D(b) *tick one box*

  are enclosed [ ]   will be sent later [✓]   are not due [ ]

- completed forms P9D (except for employees for whom you have already completed forms P11D) for payments and benefits described on form P9D *tick one box*

  are enclosed [ ]   will be sent later [✓]   are not due [ ]

- completed forms P38A *tick one box*

  are enclosed [✓]   will be sent later [ ]   are not due [ ]

- my 'Employer's contracting out number', where applicable, as notified on the Occupational Pensions Board's Certificate is -

  E 1 2 4 5 7 8 9 0

I claim a payment under Section 7 of the Social Security Act 1986 for each employee on whose End of Year Return I have entered a scheme contracting-out number. So far as I know each of them is in an employment which has not been contracted-out by reference to any other scheme since 1 January 1986.

- all the details entered on the End of Year Returns (forms P14) and required by this notice are fully and truly stated to the best of my knowledge and belief.

Signature of employer: *[signature]*
Date: 19 4 89

P35(1988)

Figure 15.3 *Employers annual statement, P35*

Source: Inland Revenue, P35

Employee's Certificate Form P60

Your employees will need to know the total amount of pay and tax deducted from their wages at the end of each tax year, and this is given to them on Form P60. This is produced as the third part of Form P14, but it is only given to employees who are in the employment on the last pay-day in the year. This means that all Forms P60 automatically produced for all employees who have left during the year can be destroyed. (It is possible to obtain a two-part P14, so that P60s need not be produced for leavers.) The form is a 'Certificate of Pay and Tax Deducted', and for this reason a duplicate is never issued. Where an employee informs you that he has lost Form P60 that you gave him, or he asks for one even though he left your employment during the year, then you should prepare a statement of pay and tax deducted, and not issue Form P60. The reason for this is that where an employee seeks a refund of tax after the end of the year, the tax office needs to be able to refer to the employer's end-of-year details, and these may take some months to be processed for all employees. Where, however, the employee produces his Certificate Form P60, then any refund can be calculated on the basis of this form.

All cash payments that have been included in gross pay for tax or NIC purposes will have been returned on Forms P14 at the end of each year. In addition, an employer will have paid out amounts in respect of reimbursed expenses or subsistence allowances, or rewarded employees by way of benefits that have not been included in gross pay on the deductions working sheet. All these items have to be returned on separate forms to the Inspector of Taxes after the year end. The deadline for submission of returns of expenses and benefits is currently 5 May, but will be extended to 19 May in line with the new deadline for Forms P35 and P14.

Form P9D

Form P9D is a return of expenses and benefits of more than £25 in a year for employees who are not directors and who have earnings for the year at less than £8500 after expenses and benefits have been included. This category of employee is taxed on a limited range of expenses and benefits only, and these are detailed on the Form P9D. An example of the completed form, with a typical benefit, is shown in Figure 15.4.

Form P11D

Form P11D is a return of expenses and benefits for directors and employees who earn at an annual rate £8500 or more, including expenses and

Inland Revenue
PAYE

Do not use this form for
employees for whom a Form
P11D is appropriate
- see overleaf.

Return of expenses payments and income from which tax cannot be deducted

Year 6 April 1988 to 5 April 1989

You are required to make a return on this form for every employee (other than those for whom a Form P11D is appropriate) to whom expenses payments have been made or benefits in kind have been provided.

Notes to help you complete this form are given overleaf but if you have difficulty in completing the form, or if you need further information, your Inspector of Taxes will gladly give any necessary advice or information.

| Please complete these boxes and those items below which apply to the employee | Employer's name GREENGRASS LTD | Employer's PAYE reference P123/45678 |
| | Employee's surname and initials SUTHERLAND DOREEN | National Insurance number AZ 5 4 29 3, 1 B |

A	**Expenses payments etc.,** *include any amount paid in respect of VAT, whether or not it may be wholly or partly recovered from H.M. Customs and Excise*	
	• Amount of expenses payments included in total pay shown on the End of Year Return including any round sum allowances.	£......................
	• Amount **not included** in total pay shown on the End of Year Return if more than £25 in the year excluding reimbursement of expenses solely and necessarily incurred in the performance of the duties.	£ 55

B	**Vouchers and Credit cards**	Amount
1.	Travel and transport vouchers including season tickets.	£
2.	Gift vouchers including National Savings Certificates and Premium Bonds.	£ 50
3.	Meal vouchers which do not comply with the conditions in para F60, Employer's Guide to PAYE.	£
4.	Any other vouchers exchangeable for goods and services.	£
5.	Credit cards provided for employees and their families. *Give details of all expenses met by credit cards provided by you unless returned under a previous heading.*	£

C	**Amounts paid on behalf of the employee or given otherwise than in money and from which tax could not be deducted.**		Amount
1.	Living accommodation provided for the employee *Enter the address of the property and the greater of (a) the gross value for rating of the property or (b) the rent and insurance borne by you.*	(a)	£
		(b)	£
	Address		
2.		Employee's own National Insurance ...	£
	Employee liabilities borne by you	Employee's personal telephone bills ...	£
		Other(s)..	£
3.	Gifts in kind such as Christmas hampers, presents, etc.		£ 10
4.	Other benefits in kind not included above. *Enter their value here and give details of the benefits in the box provided overleaf.*		£

P9D (1988)

Figure 15.4 *Expenses, income and payments return form for employers*

Source: Inland Revenue, P9D

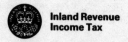

Inland Revenue
Income Tax

<table>
<tr><td>For Official use
Assessing point reference
if elsewhere</td></tr>
</table>

Employer's name   GREENGRASS LTD   PAYE reference   P123/45678

Employee's/director's name   MS NELLA PEACH   NI number   YA 06 09 00 B

Return of expenses payments and benefits etc - directors and "higher-paid" employees - year ended 5 April 1989

Please read form P11D (Guide) before completing this form.

You are required to make a return by 6 May 1989 of all expenses payments and benefits relating to -

- directors - *for certain exceptions see form P11D (Guide)*
- employees who are paid at a rate of £8,500 or more including expenses and benefits.

You should not show expenses covered by a dispensation *see form P11D (Guide).*

You are also asked to give details of certain remuneration in Part A below.

A Remuneration

1 Please give details of remuneration paid in the year to 5 April 1989 but earned in another year.

Description and period _____ Amount £ _____

B Cars and car fuel

2 **Cars made available for private use**

If more than one car made available during the year, give details of each car at (a) and (b)

Make and model (a) VAUXHALL CARLTON CD 2200cc   (b) _____ cc

	(a)	(b)
Value when new £19,250 or less	☑	☐
£19,251 - £29,000	☐	☐
more than £29,000	☐	☐
First registered on-or after 6.4.85	☑	☐
before 6.4.85	☐	☐

Made available to director/employee from 6/4/88 to 5/4/89   from _____ to _____

The amount of any wages paid to a driver provided for the director/employee in respect of private journeys £ _____

Payment received from the director/employee for the private use of the car £ _____

	Yes	"✓" No	Don't know
Was the car, to your own knowledge, used for business travel - for 2,500 miles pa or less?	☐	☑	☐
- for 18,000 miles pa or more?	☐	☑	☐

3 **Car fuel "scale charges" - cars available for private use**

	Yes	No
Was fuel for the car(s) provided other than for business travel?	☑	☐
If "yes" was the director/employee required to make good the cost of all fuel used for private motoring including travel between home and normal place of work?	☐	☑
If the director/employee was required to make good the cost did he actually do so?	☐	☐

4 **Car owned or hired by director/employee**

Allowances paid to the director/employee in respect of the use of the car and/or running and overhead expenses £ _____

Sum contributed by you towards the purchase price, depreciation or hire of a car £ _____

For official use

P11D (1988)

Printed in the UK for HMSO 12/88 Dd 8134319 4300M 25038

C Beneficial loans

5 Enter details of loans made to, or arranged for, a director/employee (or any of his relatives) on which no interest was paid or on which the amount of interest paid was less than interest at the official rate.

	Yes	No	Don't know
(a) Were there any loans the interest on which was (or would have been if interest had been payable) not wholly eligible for relief?	☐	☐	☐
(b) If the answer to (a) is "yes" did the benefit of the loans exceed £200?	☐	☐	☐

(c) *Unless you have answered "No" to (b)* -

- add all the loans together and state the total amounts outstanding at 5.4.88 _____ at 5.4.89 _____

- If the loan was made on or after 6 April 1988 state the amount and the date it was paid. £ _____ Date _____

- If the loan was discharged on or before 5 April 1989 on what date was it discharged? Date _____

- What was the amount of interest paid by the borrower in the year to 5 April 1989 £ _____
  Enter "NIL" if none was paid.

(d) If any loans made by you were waived or written off in the year to 5 April 1989 what was the amount waived etc? £ _____

D Other expenses payments and benefits etc

		£
6 Private medical dental etc attention and treatment or insurance against the cost of such treatment BUPA		150—
7 General expenses allowance		1695—
8 Travelling and subsistence		
9 Entertainment		
10 Home telephone	Rental	68.—
	Calls	195—
11 Subscriptions SUMMERTOWN TENNIS CLUB		25—
12 Goods or services supplied free or below market value		
13 Vouchers and credit cards		
14 Cars, property, furniture and other assets given or transferred to the director/employee		
15 Educational assistance provided for the director/employee or members of his family		
16 House, flat or other living accommodation provided for the director/employee		
Please show address _____ Cost £ _____		
17 Income tax paid to the Collector in the year to 5 April 1989 which a company failed to deduct from a director's remuneration		
18 Other expenses and benefits not shown above eg National Insurance contributions, holidays, private legal, accountancy etc expenses, nursery facilities, contributions towards house purchase, rates and other household expenses such as wages and keep of personal or domestic staff and gardening expenses.		
Please give details _____		

	Total	2133—
Less (i) So much of the items entered above as have been made good by the director/employee	+ _____	
(ii) Amounts included above from which tax has been deducted under PAYE	=	68—
	Net total	2065—

Declaration

I declare that all particulars required are fully and truly stated according to the best of my knowledge and belief.

Signature _____ Date 30/4/89

Capacity in which signed _____DIRECTOR_____

Figure 15.5 *Employer's form for return of expenses payments and benefits*

Source: Inland Revenue, P11D

benefits. The £8500 limit needs to be calculated accurately. To arrive at this figure, you need to add together gross pay, after deducting ordinary superannuation or pension contributions, all expenses payments including those paid direct by you, all benefits including car and car fuel scale charges, and any items of expense to do with the car that are met by vouchers or credit cards, or by paying the employee's bills, and any items of expense or benefit from any related business for which the employee also works (see Figure 15.5).

Form P11D should be examined very carefully, as it is in this area that many employers fail to make a full return of all the benefits they provide for their employees. The excuse will normally be one of ignorance: 'Surely the form is not meant to apply to a loan for a season ticket', but there are penalties for either not completing a form for a relevant employee, or for failure to complete the form correctly. The penalty for a wrong return has been increased to £3000 in the 1989 Finance Act, and relates to each employee. This means that for an employer with 100 employees the maximum penalty for incorrect returns could be £300,000!

Employers need to consider that anything of value which they provide for employees, if it is not cash and included in gross pay for tax purposes, is very likely to be a benefit that should be recorded on Form P11D. There are very few exceptions to this rule. Because of the complexities of the form and the legislation involved, many employers seek professional advice for the completion of these returns.

Start of a new tax year

At the same time as employers are preparing all the end-of-year returns, the new tax year will be starting and new deductions working sheets Form P11 will need to be prepared for each employee. Before the start of the new tax year, the Inspector of Taxes will send an Employer's Pack, which may contain new codes for some of the employees. These new codes should be operated from the first pay-day in the new year. The pack will also contain reminders about the PAYE threshold and the correct emergency code.

Where a new code has not been received for an employee, you should carry forward the code which you used in the old tax year. But where a 'week 1' or 'month 1' instruction was noted, this can be deleted.

Part Five:
Moving To A Computerised System

16

Do You Really Need to Computerise Your Payroll?

Introduction

The first things an employer will need to take into account if he is considering computerising payroll is whether the business is already using a computer for stock control, accounts or some other function. If it is, then it may be necessary only to invest in payroll software. If, however, there is no computer function at all in the business then the employer, assuming that he decides computerisation is really to his advantage and that the firm can afford it, will have to purchase both hardware (ie computer, Visual Display Units (VDUs), printers etc) and software (ie program disks etc).

Computers are ideal for making mathematical calculations very quickly and for storing data. For payroll purposes this is ideal because there are complicated calculations to be done each pay period and a host of data has to be retained for each employee, including names and addresses, personal details and matters relating to rates of pay, overtime, commission, holiday pay, travel expenses, etc. Employers are often led into thinking that a computer system will fulfil all their expectations, but this is far from being the case. Important decisions have to be made before wages can be paid, and computers cannot be programmed to make many of these decisions. A trained payroll person will always be required to decide who is an employee, which payments are subject to tax and National Insurance Contributions (NIC), when the payments should be made and all the other decisions of principle in the very complicated statutory systems imposed by the Inland Revenue and the Department of Social Security (DSS). Once the decisions have been made and the information fed into the computer, then the recording and retrieval of information is speeded up many times, as are all the calculation procedures.

Who needs a computerised system?

In simple terms an employer will benefit from a computerised system where the cost of manually calculating and processing the payroll will exceed the cost of an equivalent computerised system. An employer with five employees could hardly achieve any economies of scale but an employer with 50,000 employees certainly would. Somewhere in between will be the optimum point for an average employer, depending upon the complexity of his existing payments systems and the range and scale of his workforce.

There are, however, other factors to be considered. It may well be that the computerisation of payroll can be carried out at the same time as the computerisation of other business functions. These could include the personnel records system, a training programme, the monitoring of sickness and absence, and a whole range of business applications such as stock control, ledger accounts and other financial records.

People buy computers for many reasons, not all of them business-orientated or even rational. It may be that the latest hardware is manufactured in a colour which matches the new decor, or everybody else in the wine bar has the latest PC and surely your business can afford one as well. There is, of course, a national perception that a business without a computer these days is still in the Dickensian era. Whatever the reason for choosing to computerise payroll, any business should take great care to ensure as far as possible that the system purchased does do what the business wants it to do.

There are a number of factors to be taken into account and this chapter will deal with the main topics that should be considered before a computer system is installed. Most businesses will find that once they ask a person or a group of people to prepare a report on computerisation, the whole issue seems to be self-generating and in a matter of weeks a range of data is available for consideration.

Requirements of the system

It is not uncommon for someone unconnected with payroll to decide on the kind of system that the payroll office needs. It can be seen from the rest of this book that payroll is a complicated matter and only someone with a knowledge of its functions can help to define what is required. It can be worthwhile for a business at this stage to bring in a consultant with good communications skills and detail to him the exact requirements of your proposed computer system, especially if it is to be multi-functional. For a system that is purely for payroll, the following factors will have to be considered:

- the number of employees now and the likely number in, say, five years' time;

- the different intervals of payment applicable to groups of people;
- the range of payments made, eg salary, wages, overtime, bonus, commission, expenses, multiple hourly rates, etc;
- the different types of payment methods currently used and those likely to be used in five years' time;
- whether staff turnover is great in relation to the number of staff employed.

This list is by no means exhaustive, and a report of what any payroll office is currently required to do, and what it may be required to do in the future, will normally amount to a weighty document. If this report is thoroughly considered and accurately put together it can be used when evaluating systems available in the market place and could even be presented to a software house with the question 'Can your system do all that?' (A reply in the affirmative should be sought in writing!)

Justification of costs

Cost is not the only factor governing the decision to invest in a computerised system, nevertheless it should be very carefully considered. A cynical business person will accept with some caution a report on cost justification that assumes that any computer system can be set up without encountering a whole range of expensive problems. Cost/benefit savings are very likely, however, to be achieved in the following areas:

- numbers of payroll staff can be significantly reduced;
- greatly reduced payroll processing time;
- accuracy and reliability of calculations;
- controlled access to private data through security systems;
- fast input, sorting and retrieval of information;
- non-paper storage of records, saving expenditure on paper and storage space;
- automatic production of reports, summaries and all end-of-year documents.

The costs incurred in setting up the new system will include the following:

- hardware and software including all new computer stationery;
- development and set-up costs using in-house and outside consultants;
- cost of time used in running and checking parallel systems;
- training of new and existing staff.

The more employees you have the greater the cost benefit will be. Once a new system is up and running efficiently, thousands of payroll calculations can be done in the time previously spent doing a few manually.

Computerisation and payroll staff

Human-beings are very often resistant to any kind of change and payroll people are no different. It is in the nature of payroll work that it requires reliability, conscientiousness and the ability to adhere strictly to deadlines – qualities which, coupled with the repetitive nature of the job each week, may sometimes mean that this section of the work-force is more resistant to change than other departments. It is recommended therefore that the payroll people are consulted and communicated with at all levels in any changeover process, and that they are treated as the experts they undoubtedly are in the payroll field.

Payroll staff will very quickly realise that there may be job losses in their department, and this can lead to considerable insecurity from the time the computer is first mentioned until it is installed. The installation of the system from the moment it is fully thought of to the time when it is up and running, can be several months, indeed it could run into years. This fact should be communicated to the payroll staff. Natural wastage would account for a reduction in number of staff members. It is possible these days to obtain agency staff or consultants who are familiar with payroll in many applications, and these people could be used to fill any gaps until the system is fully operational and staff numbers level out. The human factors to be considered in installing a computerised system are as follows:

- the user-friendliness of the system;
- attitudes of staff to new technology;
- short-term and long-term effects on payroll staffing;
- consultation with all levels of staff in the planning and implementation;
- training programmes;
- changes that may be necessary in contracts of employment or conditions of service;
- consultation with trade unions concerning effects upon the whole workforce.

Compatibility

If a business already has a computer function, then it is always worthwhile investigating whether any new system will be required to exchange data with an existing one, and if so to ensure that the two systems are compatible. Always specify in writing to supply companies, the precise details of any existing system and ask for confirmation in writing that the existing and new systems will be compatible in specified areas. Buying a computer system seems to be like buying a car, in that once it is seen that the outside looks very nice, people tend to assume that the bit under the bonnet will work. It is worth attempting to draw up terms of reference with outside contractors to try to ensure that what they say they will do, they actually achieve.

Businesses will need to consider a number of factors here, including the types of magnetic tape used in existing functions and whether these tapes will be suitable for payroll, and indeed whether appropriate data can be produced for use if the Bankers' Automated Clearing System (BACS) is used for payment of wages.

Most software houses should be able to give you 'reference points', which means they have satisfied customers whom they are prepared to disclose to potential new customers. This means that you can go and view. a number of the systems you are considering purchasing and see them operating in a real situation. It is worthwhile visiting these sites, but you should try to have discussions with several levels of personnel. A computer programmer may have had a wonderful time setting up a new system and be thoroughly pleased with all the exciting new items. You will, however, also need to interview the end-users, ie the payroll clerks, and ask them whether the system actually does what it promised to do. It is worth establishing which areas of the business receive reports from the system, for example the company's accounts and personnel departments, and finding out from them whether the reports received were what was required.

In addition to the reference sites offered by the software house it is common for the larger payroll systems to have 'user groups'. It should be relatively simple to find the address of the user group secretary and ask for a list of his members, or at least a selection you may be able to contact. In this way you will be able to get feedback from a variety of companies, not just the ones that the software house initially offer for reference.

Planning and time-scales

The change to a computerised payroll system may take years rather than months to achieve, so clearly careful planning is needed to achieve the best result in the shortest possible time. Normally a programme of events will be prepared covering the whole project, which may need adjustment from time to time. In simple terms, it is little use buying the software at the beginning if the hardware is not to be delivered for six months.

Inevitably the changeover from manual to a fully computerised system is a complicated and time-consuming business. The changeover needs to be controlled carefully at all stages, so that the costs of setting up the new system are not greatly exceeded before any benefits are reaped.

17
Selecting Suitable Hardware and Software

Introduction

If the fullest possible planning, including assessment and specification, has been undertaken, it will be easier to detemine the type of computer system required. If at this point you decide to look at what is on the market you will be deluged with a host of systems, from micros or PCs, minis, to mainframes and even the bureau option. It is worthwhile considering this last option before any of the others. Under the bureau system, another business provides all the hardware and software for you at their place of business, but your payroll staff still have to tell it what to do.

Using a bureau

A number of companies around the country operate bureau systems for payroll. Some of these businesses have arisen out of the spare capacity of an existing payroll system, and pieces of this capacity have been sold off to other businesses. In recent years the trend is for specialised payroll bureaux to be set up and they have developed a range of expertise in the complicated payroll area.

Generally, a bureau will have all the equipment needed, so that all the input of data for each pay period – the calculation procedures, the production of reports, summaries, payslips, etc – can be processed by the bureau and copies sent back to the client business. This means, however, that you would need to have payroll staff trained not only in basic payroll procedures but also in the completion of the input documents supplied by that bureau. A bureau will normally ascertain the precise facilities required by a business for its payroll system, eg the number of employees and the range of payments and pay intervals, and quote a price per payslip produced with normally a minimum charge. These bureaux are in the main reliable and efficient, will save all the capital cost of a new payroll system, and the changeover time can be very much shorter than setting up your own system. Bureaux have shown that they often have a viable solution for businesses whether their employees number just a handful or several hundreds.

In-house system

The payroll office was in fact one of the first business areas to use computers, because the calculations were such that they could be easily computerised. Indeed, other types of business machines were firstly used in the payroll office. This led to large employers producing their own customised computer payroll system which was updated each year by their own programmers. For many years this was a straightforward answer, but as the tax and National Insurance Contributions (NIC) systems became more complicated, and following the introduction of Statutory Sick Pay (SSP) and Statutory Maternity Pay (SMP), together with the added complications of new pension legislation, the annual update of the systems became a very expensive and time-consuming operation. Few businesses today have the resources to keep continually up to date an in-house payroll system.

There is available a whole range of software payroll systems for purchase or lease which can either be used virtually 'off the peg' or which are customised to suit the needs of individual payroll offices. These systems are now so sophisticated that it would not be worth the company investing resources in 'reinventing the wheel'.

Purchasing software

There is a whole range of payroll packages available on software and these range from those suitable for micro or mini systems through PC and mainframe computers. The choice will depend largely upon the desired level of compatibility with other computer facilities within the company. The differences in these systems will be of cost, speed of processing, storage capacity and facilities for connection of terminals, printers, etc. The main points about these different systems are shown below.

1. *Mainframe.* The initial cost of purchasing a mainframe computer will be relatively large, but the processing capacity should cope not only with payroll but all other computer facilities a company would need. They are usually centrally based, so that it is possible for sites around the country to link into this central unit. The large capacity will cope with a payroll of thousands, and allow interface between other related functions, such as personnel and accounts.

2. *Mini computers.* The latest ranges of these kind of computers have greatly increased capacities, and the largest can now cope with payrolls of considerable size. There is, in addition, a greater range of payroll software available in this range that would be sufficiently complex to cope with the many features required by a larger payroll. A number of terminals can be connected to the main terminal so that not only can more than one person use the system, but it is also possible for different people to use different applications, for example payroll, personnel or pension systems at the same time.

3. *Personal computers (PCs).* The storage capacity of some of these machines is somewhat limited, so they would normally be suitable for small payrolls only. Older models of 'stand alone' PCs can be used within the payroll office but there is no facility at present for multiple use; in other words, on the day when payroll information is being processed it would not be possible to process an accounting or other function without changing programmes. The new models of PCs can be connected to a mainframe, and can access data from this, and can also be connected to PCs in a 'network'.

   There are a number of software packages available for PCs, but here again the range of facilities available varies and may be less than you would obtain in a mainframe or mini system. Many of the small payroll systems for PCs (which are relatively inexpensive) require the user to have already worked out gross pay, pension contributions or amounts of SSP, and feed these into the system so that tax and NI can be calculated. The latest programs for networked PCs contain most features of a mainframe system.

Many companies are now in the payroll software business, and once a company shows that it is in the market for a system, it is likely to be deluged with literature and visiting sales people. Most of the literature will be too general and will not be able to give a precise indication of all the facilities of that system, therefore more information will be gleaned from the presentations and demonstrations given by sales people.

The selling of computer hardware and software is a sophisticated business, and you will find that on occasions quite lavish demonstrations will be arranged to woo you towards a range of products. Most sales people will have been thoroughly trained in the system that they are selling, but it would be unusual for them to be either programmers or users of any system. They will encourage you to ask questions, but the replies given should be assessed against the likely level of in-depth knowledge of a system. You should be able to establish this with a few questions, such as 'Have you personally ever used this system?' or 'Have you personally ever worked in a payroll office or been involved with the actual set-up of such a system?' You will very often be given demonstrations of the system which will show many of its features, perhaps a video of the company with members of its staff and premises, and even interviews with the satisfied customers. It is at this stage that asking for a reference site could be useful, and visits to the suggested sites, or other end-users whom you can establish from the user group, and who should be able to give a much fuller picture of how well the system actually functions.

18

Setting Up and Running Your Computerised System

Introduction

When the decision has been taken to computerise payroll (and any other areas of the business) and the most suitable hardware and software systems, or the bureau option, have been chosen, there will be a period during which the system can be got 'up and running'. This time will vary from weeks to months, depending upon the size and complexity of your system. The main areas to be considered, and their approximate order are as follows.

Site preparation

Where hardware is to be purchased, then suitable accommodation for it will need to be prepared. The kinds of things which will need to be considered are heating and lighting, air conditioning, conduits for cable laying, fire precautions and noise levels. In addition there will be the rooms in which the users will work, and where terminals or Visual Display Units (VDUs) and also printers will be housed. Consideration must be given to the layout of this room, any special furniture, including chairs for VDU operators will need to be purchased, and any special lighting to minimise glare from screens. You should consult the Health and Safety at Work Act to ensure that the new layout for equipment will be safe for use by all persons concerned.

At the planning stage, the security precautions for the accommodation areas should be looked at carefully. You would normally require limited access to your computer hardware and software because of the kinds of records that would be maintained in any payroll office. You may also consider setting up a modern entry system to control access to specific key areas.

Equipment installation

Hardware suppliers will have informed you of the delivery period, so that planning can be made to ensure that the accommodation will be ready. They will deliver not just to site but to the exact location, and will carry out the necessary wiring and test procedures. These suppliers should have been consulted in the discussions regarding the siting of the equipment security, etc.

Software installation

You should expect to receive a certain amount of assistance from the software house, often in the form of an installation engineer or consultant, at no extra cost. Any additional consultancy time in helping you set up your system is normally charged for.

It is at this stage that you will need the original document that was drawn up to specify the requirements of your system, so that your in-house programmers are fully aware of the number and range of the facilities that your users require. It is not uncommon for programmers to look at a complicated payroll process, decide that payroll would never use it, and therefore not set it up. There are many cases where users, when informed that some complicated calculation, for example of Statutory Sick Pay (SSP) or National Insurance (NI) on holiday pay can be carried out by the system, say that they were unaware that the system could do this.

As the setting up of the software progresses, it should be possible to print out each section of the programme, in order to check the input one section at a time. Small errors in setting up can, of course, affect thousands of calculations. The programmers should be communicating with the users throughout this period to help prevent any later problems that will take longer to rectify. When the software installation is completed, it should be possible to set up and run a test programme so that input of data, the calculations processed and the output can be thoroughly checked.

Data input

It takes time to set up all the data necessary for a payroll system, and the process should not be hurried. You must aim for the correctness of the data because if at the end of this set-up process a number of errors are discovered, you may be unable to estimate the scale of the errors, which may necessitate the checking of every single item of data. Here again print-outs should be obtained for each batch of data input, and checks made. It will not be just personal data such as names and addresses and rates of pay that need to be set up, but the 'skeleton' of the system, encompassing such things as frequency and methods of payments, ranges of bonus and overtime scales relating to your particular business.

You will need to decide who is to input this data, and when it is to be done. In most cases the existing payroll staff will want to be involved, but this will mean that their main duties of running the current payroll may not receive their full attention. This area of overlap will need to be planned, with the possibility of taking on temporary staff to cover this period.

Test and parallel runs

It is sometimes possible to programme the installation of a new payroll procedure so that the changeover time can be when the tax year ends on 5 April. This means that the old year can be finalised on the old system and all the data can be ready to process week or month 1 on the new system. It is advisable, however, to run both systems parallel for a short period to compare all the calculations and outputs. This should bring to your attention any 'bugs' in the system. It should be at this stage that everyone involved in the changeover can stand back in amazement at the speed and efficiency of the new system!

All systems go

When all the checks have been made on the new system, and any bugs removed, it should be possible to use the new system 100 per cent for payroll processes. No new system will run perfectly without problems from time to time, but these are usually easy to solve by referring to the 'trouble-shooting' part of the manuals which are given with the system, or by telephoning the software suppliers. Software houses usually have quite large customer support divisions, which is an indication that they are necessary and frequently used by their customers. The customer services departments should give sufficient advice and support at any time, so that your payroll will be produced on time.

Data protection

The 1984 Data Protection Act introduced certain requirements for companies who use computers to process personal data. A payroll system is a prime user of personal data, and although payroll systems may be exempt from the provisions to some extent, companies are advised to investigate thoroughly whether registration under the Data Protection Act is required. In the first instance you should obtain the eight booklets containing 'Data Protection Guidelines'.

- *Guideline 1 Introduction to the Act*
- *Guideline 2 The Definitions*
- *Guideline 3 The Register and Registration*
- *Guideline 4 The Data Protection Principle*
- *Guideline 5 Individuals' Rights*
- *Guideline 6 The Exceptions*
- *Guideline 7 Enforcement and Appeals*
- *Guideline 8 Summary for Computer Bureaux.*

These booklets are available, free of charge, from:

The Registrar's Enquiry Service
Springfield House
Water Lane
Wilmslow
Cheshire
SK9 5AX
(Tel: (0625) 535777).

Index

Page numbers in italic refer to illustrations.